CW00841558

MAGIC MUSHROOMS

A GUIDE TO CULTIVATION

AND SAFE USE

HANK BRYANT AND

ISRAEL BOUSEMAN

1st Edition, published in 2019
© 2019 by Monkey Publishing
Monkey Publishing
Lerchenstrasse 111
22767 Hamburg
Germany

Published by *Monkey Publishing*
Edited by *Lily Marlene Booth*
Cover Design by *Diogo Lando*
Cover Image by *Elena Yakusheva/Shutterstock*
Graphics on Title & Publisher Page:
Mis-Tery, Irina Skalaban/Shutterstock.com
Printed by *Amazon**

ISBN: 9781095433720

All rights reserved. No part of this publication may be reproduced or transmitted in any form or by any mean, electronic or mechanical, including photocopying, recording, or by any information storage and retrieval system, without permission in writing form. Reviewers may quote brief passages.

This book contains information on growing psilocybin mushrooms: it has been written and published with the intention of offering information to the public. Psilocybin is an illegal substance throughout much of the world. The publisher does not advocate the practice of illegal activities and advises the reader to conduct their own research in order to gain a thorough understanding of the legal restrictions that may apply to them. Although the author and publisher have made every effort to ensure that the information in this book was correct at press time, the author and publisher do nat assume and hereby disclaim any liability to any party for any loss, damage, or disruption caused by errors or omissions, whether such errors or omissions result from negligence, accident, or any other cause.

*printed by Amazon in the country the customer has placed the order.

GET MY NEW BOOK ON PSILOCYBIN MUSHROOM IDENTIFICATION FOR FREE

I'm currently searching for reviewers for my newest book on **Psilocybin Mushroom Identification**. Since you have purchased this book, I'm wondering if you let me provide you with a free advanced copy of my new book in hopes you consider reviewing it? Your interest in Magic Mushrooms and being a savvy reader would make you a perfect candidate to provide the quality feedback I'm searching for.

If you would be interested, I'm happy to send you a free digital copy.

You can sign-up for the reviewer list here:
https://psilocybin.gr8.com/

Of course, I understand that you are under zero obligations to review my book, and if you do review it, all I ask is that you leave an honest review on Amazon once the book is launched. It would be a great pleasure to have you involved in the project.

Thank you very much for your consideration and have a wonderful day!

Hank
Author & Shrooms Enthusiast

REASONS FOR WRITING THIS BOOK

The use of psychedelics in many forms has been a part of human culture since the stone age. Psilocybin mushrooms and other hallucinogenic substances have been employed by shamans of many cultures to aid in journeying. In a number of cultures, the use of these substances formed an essential part of spiritual practice.

In the modern era, though psilocybin mushrooms and other hallucinogens are still heavily regulated or downright illegal, although the medical and scientific community are beginning to recognize the therapeutic benefits of the psychedelic experience. Recent research has suggested that psilocybin, one of the main psychedelic compounds in magic mushrooms, has been effective in treating cluster headaches, depression, mood and anxiety disorders, addiction, and obsessive compulsive disorder. And these are just a few of the potential therapeutic benefits. Current studies also suggest that psilocybin and other psychedelics have the potential to rewire the brain itself, facilitating positive, long-term personal transformation.

One of the greatest things about this is that mushrooms are 100% natural and fairly easy to cultivate. With this in mind, one of my main motivations in writing this book is to spread knowledge about these techniques and bring cultivation within reach for anyone interested in journeying with psilocybin mushrooms. Not only are they safe, but they are also able to be grown by anyone who really wishes to do so. So, here is an in-depth exploration suitable for beginners and advanced cultivators alike.

Yellowj/Shutterstock.com

It is my opinion that psychedelics are some of the greatest learning tools we have ever encountered. Furthermore, I believe they should be treated with respect, with a full understanding of what they have to offer and how they can best be used. Psilocybin mushrooms and other hallucinogenic plants are amazing teachers if approached correctly. In writing this, I hope to spread awareness regarding the potential of the psychedelic experience and to help those interested in the subject to make more informed choices, specifically regarding the safe use and cultivation of these teachers.

GHED/Shutterstock.com

This book is divided into four parts. The first part addresses the **psilocybin experience and safe use**. The second part, beginning with chapter 7, focuses on the **basics of mushroom cultivation**. In part three, beginning with chapter 11, we move from theory to action and provide you with the **practical skills to grow your own mushrooms**. We'll talk about the equipment and materials you are going to need, then give **step-by-step instructions for five different cultivation methods** or "Teks." Chapter 13 gives advanced techniques for **propagating your own cultures**, from collecting spores and **making your own spore and mycelial syringes** to germinating mycelium on agar, grain and cardboard, plus **cloning techniques** and finally ways for **long-term storage of**

7

your cultures. In the last part, the **legality** of psilocybin mushrooms will be discussed in a number of contexts and we provide some more reference sources.

The reader can either read the book straight through or go directly to the part that they are interested in. If you're just starting out with cultivation and wanting to set up your first flush, skip right to part two. If you have a bit of experience and you're ready to refine your cultivation technique, jump right into chapter 13.

Even when cultivation and use are legal in your country or state, the greatest respect should be used when working with psilocybin and other psychedelic substances. These are not recreational drugs. However, when used correctly, with due caution and proper understanding, they can have amazing benefits. It is my hope that the information presented in this book will give the reader a better awareness of how to work with psilocybin mushrooms safely and therapeutically. In particular, I hope to help the reader better understand the psychedelic experience and how it can be constructively navigated.

PART I
PSYCHEDELICS AND SAFE USE

CHAPTER 1. WHAT'S THE DEAL WITH MAGIC MUSHROOMS?

MAGIC MUSHROOMS: AN OVERVIEW

MAGIC MUSHROOMS: A HISTORY

EARLY USE OF PSILOCYBIN

PSILOCYBIN MUSHROOMS IN WESTERN SOCIETY

Chapter 1. What's the Deal with Magic Mushrooms?

Magic Mushrooms: An Overview

Magic mushrooms, also known as 'shrooms, are any of several mushroom species which contain psychedelic (hallucinogenic) compounds. There are two main types of hallucinogenic mushrooms: amanita and psilocybin. However, this book will focus exclusively on the latter, as the Amanita genus contains a number of extremely deadly species which can be difficult for the novice to distinguish from the purely psychedelic species.

Wakajawaka/Shutterstock.com

There are more than 180 species of psilocybin mushrooms. More than 100 of these species are in the genus Psilocybe. However, a number of species come from other genera including Pluteus, Pholiotina, Mycena, Inocybe, Galerina, Copelandia, Gymnopilus, and Conocybe. The structure and appearance of each species are distinct, and they appear in specific regions. Therefore, great care should be taken when attempting to identify mushrooms, especially in unfamiliar regions. All of these mushrooms are known as psilocybin mushrooms, as psilocybin is one of the main psychoactive compounds they contain. Two other psychoactive compounds have been identified in psilocybin mushrooms: psilocin and baeocystin. When ingested, these mushrooms induce a psychedelic experience. This experience brings about an altered state of consciousness alongside changes in sensory perception.

Psilocybin mushrooms grow all over the world, with different species native to different regions. They can be found on all continents except Antarctica, though most species tend to prefer subtropical and tropical regions. These mushrooms have a long history of use in the tribes of Central and South America for religious and spiritual rituals. In modern times, they are one of the most commonly-used recreational hallucinogens in Europe and the United States.

MAGIC MUSHROOMS: A HISTORY

One of the most compelling things about psilocybin mushrooms is that the history of their use goes back to the very dawn of humanity. As far back as we look, and in societies all across the globe, we can find signs of their use. There are even some compelling theories about their role in our evolution as a civilized species. While this is conjecture as yet, it's fascinating to explore our historical relationship with this gentle and powerful organism.

EARLY USE OF PSILOCYBIN

Though we don't know when humans first discovered psychoactive mushrooms, archeological findings suggest that they have been known and used by early human tribes at least 9000 years ago. Some of the earliest evidence comes from stone-age art. Depictions of mushrooms can be found in cave paintings discovered near Villa del Homo, Spain and in the Tassili caves in southern Algeria. These have led archeologists to hypothesize that early humans used psychedelic mushrooms in religious rituals.

One theory, posited by Terrence McKenna, is that psychedelic mushrooms were a central influence in human evolution. McKenna has posited that magic mushrooms helped to raise human consciousness to the level of self-reflection and abstract thought. This theory has been criticized by the scientific community as being lacking in evidence. However, current studies into the impact of psychedelics on brain function suggest that they have the capacity to reorganize neural connections and increase communication between different parts of the brain. To me, this suggests that there might be more to McKenna's theory than the scientific community has yet recognized.

To bring this to (relatively) more modern times, numerous stone carvings depicting mushrooms have been found in Central and South America. Many of these statues and murals date back more than 2000 years and have marked similarity to specific Psilocybe species. The Mayan, Aztec, Mazatec, Nahua, Mixtec, and Zapotec tribes of Central America are all known to have used psychedelic mushrooms in their religious rituals. The Aztecs called one Psilocybe species teonanacatl, meaning "flesh of the gods." Mazatec and Aztec names for psilocybin mushrooms can be translated to "wondrous mushrooms," "divinatory mushrooms," and "genius mushrooms."

The use of psilocybin mushrooms was prevalent amongst these tribes when the Spanish conquistadors arrived in the New World. However, the Spanish viewed their use with suspicion, believing that they allowed users to communicate with devils. Therefore, the use of Psilocybes and other psychedelic substances was suppressed. Efforts to convert the tribes to Catholicism also resulted in the suppression of all religious and spiritual traditions of the tribes. However, tribal religious practices, including those which use entheogens (psychedelic substances), have persisted, often in secret, into the present day.

PSILOCYBIN MUSHROOMS IN WESTERN SOCIETY

Western society has only encountered psychedelics relatively recently. This was largely due to Maria Sabina, a Mexican curandera, or native healer. Maria Sabina held healing rituals known as veladas. During these rituals, participants would ingest psilocybin mushrooms as a spiritual sacrament intended to purify and facilitate sacred communion. Sabina learned about the use of psilocybin mushrooms from her grandfather and great-grandfather, both shamans in the Mazatec tradition.

Valentina Wasson and R. Gordon Wasson were a married couple who were permitted by Maria Sabina to attend the velada in 1955. Their experience was so profound that they sought to make the potential of psilocybin mushrooms known to the West. Wasson collected spores from the mushrooms ingested during the ceremony. He brought these spores to Robert Heim, who, in the following year, identified them as members of the genus Psilocybe. Subsequent fieldwork allowed Heim to identify three species of Psilocybe used in the velada: Psilocybe mexicana, Psilocybe caerulescens, and Psilocybe zapotecorum. In 1957, the same year Albert Hoffman accidentally discovered LSD, Wasson published an article in *Life* Magazine entitled "Seeking the Magic Mushroom." This made Wasson's experience available, at least in printed form, to the West. By 1958, Hoffman had identified psilocybin and psilocin as psychoactive compounds in psilocybin mushrooms. In the process, Hoffman began to synthesize psilocybin, making it possible for the purified compound to be tested in Western psychological trials.

Timothy Leary, after encountering Wasson's article, visited Mexico to gain firsthand experience of the psychedelic effects of psilocybin mushrooms. Leary returned to Harvard in 1960 and partnered with Richard Alpert to begin the Harvard Psilocybin Project. This project was a forum for the study of psychedelic substances, both from a psychological and spiritual standpoint. Though it led to the dismissal of Alpert and Leary from Harvard by 1963, their work and that of other contemporary researchers exploded into the popular field.

As Leary and Alpert continued to promote the psychedelic experience in 1960's counterculture, interest grew. As it did, both the use of psilocybin mushrooms and research into them expanded. By the beginning of the next decade, several Psilocybe species had been identified throughout North America, Asia, and Europe. As these mushrooms are naturally occurring across the world, positive identification was followed by collection. During this period, a number of works were also published detailing how to cultivate Psilocybe cubensis. P. cubensis is a species of psilocybin mushroom which is extremely hardy and relatively easy to grow. This makes it a perfect specimen for cultivation by novices with limited materials.

In the present day, psilocybin mushrooms are among the most widely-used psychedelic substances. They are readily available in nature and easy to cultivate. Furthermore, they have been described in the 2017 Global Drug Survey as the safest recreational drug. Despite this, the active compounds of psilocybin mushrooms, psilocybin, and psilocin were declared in 1968 to be as illegal in their purified form as heroin and crack cocaine. Legality of the mushrooms themselves varies by country and will be discussed in greater detail in later sections.

CHAPTER 2. THINGS YOU MIGHT LIKE TO KNOW ABOUT 'SHROOMS

GENERAL INFORMATION

FACTS AND STATISTICS

CHAPTER 2. THINGS YOU MIGHT LIKE TO KNOW ABOUT 'SHROOMS

The Naked Eye/Shutterstock.com

As with anything, it helps to be informed. So, this section provides a bit of background information on psilocybin mushrooms, as well as some facts and figures associated with their use and the use of psychedelics in general.

GENERAL INFORMATION

One of the first things you might like to know about psilocybin mushrooms is that they are neither toxic nor addictive. One common myth about 'shrooms is that they are poisonous and that it is the poison which creates the psychedelic experience. This could be considered to be true—but only if you categorize poisonous substances as compounds that create an "intoxicated" or altered state. In that case, this definition would include every single drug, including caffeine and marijuana, not to mention nicotine and alcohol. However, if your definition of poisonous is something that has a toxic effect on the body, then psilocybin mushrooms do not fall into this category. In fact, they have fewer toxic effects than any of the drugs mentioned above, aside from marijuana, which has no recorded toxic effects whatsoever.

Magic mushrooms do not cause any known major health effects. They do not, as another myth suggests, cause bleeding of the brain or stomach. Nor do they cause kidney failure. A 1981 report found no complication of mushroom use in healthy individuals aside from dilated pupils and overly sensitive reflexes during the period of the trip.

Furthermore, you are not likely to overdose, as the typical "heroic" or massive dose is about 5g of dried mushrooms. To even get close to your limit for overdosing, you'd have to consume about 1.7kg of dried mushrooms. Quickly. And have your body process the whole lot pretty much instantaneously. For the Americans out there, that's about 3 ¾lb of dried mushrooms. Which, if you're curious, comes to about 17kg or 37.5lb of fresh mushrooms. Bottom line–it's not going to happen. (For the math geeks out there, this means that dried mushrooms are 10x more potent than fresh mushrooms by weight. Taken a step further, this means that 90% of the weight of fresh mushrooms comes from water.)

Despite being categorized amongst highly illegal drugs with no known therapeutic use and a high potential for abuse, psilocybin has very little potential for abuse. In fact, it has been shown to be helpful in the treatment of addiction. Furthermore, tolerance develops very quickly with psilocybin and other psychedelic substances, making it extremely difficult to abuse them chronically. And, should this elicit concern, this tolerance also drops within a couple of days after use. A rule of thumb with psychedelics is that, should you choose to trip two days in a row, on the second day, you will have to ingest double the amount of the first day to have the same effect. It makes a lot more sense just to space out your trips.

The same applies to situations where you would like to extend the period of the trip. Often, taking more hallucinogens after you have peaked will produce a longer trip, but will not increase the intensity unless a much larger dose is ingested. Before you follow this rule blindly, remember that each person's body chemistry is different. Plus, with psilocybin mushrooms, it is difficult to estimate the exact dose, so it is preferable to proceed with caution.

Another common fear is that psilocybin mushrooms and other psychedelics will make you go insane. This is simply not the case. However, they do bring on an intensity of emotion and experience. When first exploring hallucinogens, it is of the utmost importance to have an experienced guide who can provide a touchstone during more intense moments. It is also important to begin with small doses until you know how your body–and your mind–will react to the experience.

If you have never tripped before and you are considering the experience, first make sure that you choose to trip with people that you are comfortable with, those that you trust completely and feel safe around. Make sure that the setting is controlled, like a nice quiet, clean place inside where you can lie down if you feel like it, or a peaceful setting outside where you can be yourself and feel close to nature. It might sound like a good idea to trip and go to a club or a party, but if you are inexperienced, these things are almost never quite as fun as you think they'll be. Find out how it will affect you first. You'll thank yourself later.

When first delving into psilocybin or other hallucinogens, one thing that you will want to remember–and maybe have reminded to you–is that you are *not* crazy and that you will *not* be like this for the rest of your life. The trip will come up, and it will come down, and you will feel normal again. In the meantime, just breathe. If you have things coming up, let them come up. Don't resist. Look at what they have to show you and file them away for later. There's no need to make major decisions while you are in that space. That's for later.

There are two major things that you might want to be cautious about when working with psilocybin mushrooms. The first is that you want to know for certain that the mushrooms you ingest are indeed psilocybin mushrooms and not some other look-alike species. This means that you don't want to go out and gather mushrooms based on pictures that you found in a book or online. That includes this book or any other. If you do plan to gather wild mushrooms, it is essential to do so with an **experienced** person who has gathered–and ingested–mushrooms in the area that you are gathering. **Experienced** means not just once or twice, but enough times that you know they're not just rolling the dice.

The second thing is that, while mushrooms and other psychedelics are not toxic, if you take more than you're accustomed to, you may decide to do something stupid, or something that makes perfect sense at the time, but which you would look at under other circumstances and feel that it may not have been a wise idea. Having a trusted guide or sitter can help to make sure that this doesn't happen. Experience is also helpful in this regard, as is choosing your moment. For example, tripping while driving or operating heavy machinery is never a good idea. Neither is darting across lanes of traffic or seeing if you have suddenly developed the ability to fly or do backflips. Perhaps you have, but let yourself come down before you test the notion.

The trip itself will begin from 20 minutes to an hour after you have ingested the mushrooms. From that point, the experience will usually last between four and six hours. It is advisable to take a day prior to the experience to get clear about your intentions and reflect a bit about where you are in life. And, it's equally advisable to give yourself a day afterward to integrate what you have experienced. This also gives you time to get grounded before rushing into work or any other unpleasant necessities.

Finally, you'll often hear horror stories about "bad trips." These are not necessarily a product of the substance itself. They are, rather, instances in which anxiety or other mental disorders are enhanced and allowed to run wild. It's to be noted that you should not use psilocybin if you have a family history of schizophrenia or if you have any known mental health issues. The drug can trigger psychotic episodes. Where you might hear of psilocybin being used for therapeutic purposes for problems such as anxiety or PTSD, this is under strict clinical conditions and with medical supervision. Please do not try it on your own.

If you don't have these problems, just relax and breathe, you'll be fine. In fact, if you cultivate a habit of relaxing deeply into the trip and surrendering to the experiences and thoughts that come your way, you'll likely never have a "bad trip" in your life, regardless of how many times that you have a psychedelic experience.

This is, however, entirely up to you. One of the main ways that psychedelic substances teach us is by amplifying our own thoughts and feelings. If you can accept what's going on within you, you'll be fine. If you try to run from it, distract yourself, numb out, or generally escape yourself in any way, you will find that it just doesn't work. We can never really get away from ourselves. Placing ourselves in these situations–**in safe settings**–can help us learn to sit with ourselves and cultivate a deep sense of self-acceptance.

Safe use will be described in much greater detail in a subsequent section.

FACTS AND STATISTICS

Here are several psilocybin facts and statistics which were drawn from a wide range of studies:

1. In one recent study, 83% of people agreed that their experience of psilocybin mushrooms in the study was one of the five most significant experiences of their lives.
2. In a survey, 94% of those who had taken psilocybin mushrooms stated that the experience was life-altering in a positive way.
3. Psilocybin pilot studies at Johns Hopkins University have suggested that psilocybin therapy may be helpful in overcoming addiction to nicotine.
4. 89% of those tested in yet another study rated high or moderate positive behavioral changes after an experience with psilocybin. These rates were consistent even after more than a year of follow-up study.
5. A 2014 MRI study on the neural impact of psilocybin showed simultaneous activity in areas like the hippocampus and anterior cingulate cortex, areas of the brain for which activity is not coordinated in typical waking consciousness. A similar study found a "dramatic change" in brain organization, where different parts of the brain communicated and synchronized with one another beyond what can be observed in typical brain function.
6. A 2011 study which measured the impact of psilocybin on the Big Five domains of personality (neuroticism, extroversion, openness, agreeableness, and conscientiousness) found that openness increased significantly after a high-dose session and that this

quality "remained significantly higher than baseline more than one year after the session."

7. Many people report that the experience of psilocybin causes a temporary dissolution of the ego. A 2017 study suggests that this temporary loss of ego could be helpful in constructively re-engineering our worldview. Furthermore, those who have gone through this experience retain flexibility of subjective perspective beyond what is observed in those who have never had a psychedelic experience.

8. Another study showed that mice given psilocybin mushrooms were less likely to freeze up in fearful situations compared to the control group. As a result of these studies, researchers are considering the potential of psilocybin for the treatment of PTSD.

9. In a study of drug rehabilitation centers of West and Central Europe, hallucinogens were found to be the least frequently seen drug. They accounted for only 0.3% of treatment requests.

10. A 2016 study found that 84% of those who had taken psychedelic drugs within their lifetime did so to learn more about themselves, 60% took psychedelics to gain spiritual understanding, and 36% did so to help in dealing with emotional issues.

CHAPTER 3. PHARMACOLOGY AND EFFECTS

PSILOCYBIN PHARMACOLOGY AND BIOCHEMISTRY

PSYCHEDELIC EFFECTS (INTERNAL EXPERIENCE)

SENSORY PSYCHEDELIC EFFECTS

EMOTIONAL PSYCHEDELIC EFFECTS

MENTAL PSYCHEDELIC EFFECTS

CHAPTER 3. PHARMACOLOGY AND EFFECTS

One of the things you'll want to know about before delving into a psilocybin experience is what it will do to you, both on the chemical and pharmacological level and on the level of internal experience. So, here's a breakdown:

PSILOCYBIN PHARMACOLOGY AND BIOCHEMISTRY

Two of the main psychoactive compounds which have been identified in psilocybin mushrooms are, as mentioned above, psilocybin and psilocin. Considering the biochemistry aspect, psilocybin is indirectly responsible for the psychedelic experience, while psilocin is directly responsible. However, psilocin oxidizes quickly upon contact with the air, while psilocybin is a much more stable molecule. Furthermore, psilocybin is broken down in the body to form bioactive psilocin.

If you have worked with fresh mushrooms, then you will be familiar with the tendency for the stalks to turn a bluish color after they have been picked. This is due to the oxidation of psilocin after the outer layer of the stem has been breached. The more it blues, the higher levels of psilocin and the greater potency. Psilocin also breaks down when the mushroom is dried or heated, making psilocybin the primary active molecule in dried or cooked mushrooms or in mushroom tea, prior to ingestion. The tendency of psilocin to oxidize as mushrooms dry is responsible for the bluish or dark-purplish color that dried mushrooms will pick up around the stems and the edges of the caps.

psilocybin   serotonin

StudioMolekuul/Shutterstock.com

For the chemistry nuts out there, both psilocin and psilocybin are derived from the amino acid tryptophan. In the body, tryptophan is a precursor to serotonin, meaning that you need to have sufficient tryptophan levels for your body to create new serotonin molecules. When you ingest psilocybin, phosphatases in your digestive system cleave the phosphoryl ester bond from psilocybin, replacing it with a hydroxyl group. The resulting compound is psilocin, which is a close chemical mimic of serotonin, a neurotransmitter also known as 5-HT or 5-hydroxytryptamine.

In biological terms, psilocin is known as a serotonin agonist. In plain terms, this means that psilocin triggers our serotonin receptors, producing the same effect as if the brain was flooded with serotonin. Cognitive effects of serotonin have been associated with learning, memory, and mood. Low serotonin levels have been linked to depression and anxiety. Happiness, human contact, and the detection of abundant resources are linked to high serotonin production.

Higher levels of serotonin also stimulate dopamine, the body's natural feel-good hormone. However, drugs that stimulate dopamine directly, like heroin and cocaine, are extremely addictive. Substances that stimulate serotonin tend to have more effective feedback mechanisms which prevent the formation of addictive pathways.

To offer a bit more biochemical understanding, we can compare the effects of psilocybin and other serotonin agonists with those of SSRI's or MDMA. Our neurons all speak to one another by releasing neurotransmitters into the synaptic cleft, or the chemical space between neurons. These neurotransmitters trigger the receiving neurons, causing a minute electric charge to travel the length of the neuron to its delivery point, or the next neuron in the link. Both SSRI's and MDMA interfere with the substances that break serotonin down after it's done its job. This means that more serotonin sticks around in the synaptic cleft and continues to trigger the receiving neuron.

The downside of this is that when the brain chemistry normalizes or finds equilibrium after the active psychological influence of these drugs, it does so by making the receiving neurotransmitter less sensitive. This accounts for the depression or the period of "blah" that is often felt after a powerful MDMA experience. The serotonin is still there. It's still doing its thing, but the neurons have had the volume turned down. With serotonin agonists, however, the receiving neuron is triggered to a higher degree while the agonist (like psilocin) is present, and the brain normalizes by breaking down the agonist. This leaves your neurotransmitters less compromised in the days and weeks that follow.

Another implication of this is that serotonin agonists are not good to mix with SSRI's or MDMA. The immediate result can be intense and sometimes even pleasurable. However, the long-term effects of mixing these substances can be extremely challenging, especially in the realm of maintaining a positive mood and relief from anxiety.

PSYCHEDELIC EFFECTS (INTERNAL EXPERIENCE)

Ok. I'll preface this by saying that there's nothing that I can say that will let someone who has never tripped before know what the trip will feel like. It's like trying to describe the taste of an orange to someone who's never tried one. No matter what you say, it won't come close to the real thing. Furthermore, each trip is different, and the experience is highly dependent upon both the internal state and external environment. However, there are certain aspects and common elements of the experience which can be described, so I'll share them as best I can.

When preparing for my first psychedelic experience, I remember asking some more experienced friends what the peak would be like. One friend told me to pay attention to the moment when "everything was happening at once." In essence, the trip strips away the filters that selectively shut off our awareness of certain aspects of the experience. This means that many things will catch your attention that might have previously gone unnoticed. This could be as simple as the particular texture or color of familiar objects, the sound of words or music, the meanings or usage of words, or even simple situational contexts. There is a range of other influences, which I will divide into sensory, emotional, and mental.

SENSORY PSYCHEDELIC EFFECTS

The sensory effects can range from subtle to profound. Often, there will be a tendency to see colors more brightly and perceive a subtle motion in stationary objects. An individual experiencing psilocybin or other psychedelics may see walls or other surfaces ripple, shimmer, or breathe. There is a tendency to perceive patterns, both with eyes closed and open.

Trails and haloes are common as well. Trails are the perception of an afterimage of moving objects, while haloes are an aura or image which surrounds objects, especially light sources. In extreme instances, viewed objects may tend to melt or form into other images, often continuing to shift into yet another image. Fixed objects in a field, such as the components of facial features, may seem to be further or closer apart than normal and may seem to move around slightly while being viewed.

Often, both visual and auditory acuity will be enhanced. In addition to the visual shifts described above, sounds may seem unusually clear, presented with greater cadence and depth than under normal circumstances. This is one of the qualities which make music such a desirable experience during the trip. This same can be experienced with sounds heard in nature. You may also experience synesthesia, a mixing of the senses where sound can be seen, sight can be felt, etc. The effects are highly personal and subjective, and with experience, you may learn to elicit or diminish these sensory effects through intention and focus.

EMOTIONAL PSYCHEDELIC EFFECTS

One of the principal effects of a trip, emotionally, is for the feelings to be enhanced and amplified. This can be a pleasurable experience or a challenging one, depending on the emotions that come up in any given moment. Memories that have been long suppressed may surface, and with them, emotions that have been experienced long ago present as intensely as when you first experienced them. A sense of euphoria or giddiness might arise, especially if you are in a good place when you entered the trip. Similarly, if you are in an anxious or depressed place, these feelings can be amplified to the level of panic or despair.

This is one of the most potentially therapeutic aspects of a trip, whether it comes from the influence of psilocybin or other psychedelics. At the same time, it can be one of the most challenging aspects of the experience. Put simply, everything we experience comes from within us. It is something that we are carrying around. The trip just makes it louder and impossible to overlook. If we are prepared to feel the feeling, accept it, and move on, then we get the therapeutic benefits. We are given an opportunity to move past trauma in a fraction of the time it might take under normal circumstances. If we fight it, then we are literally put through hell. And the thing is, it's our choice if we understand that we've bought the ticket, and we're taking the ride. Once we've begun, the only way out is through.

Under the most pleasant of circumstances, all you have to do is sit back and enjoy the ride. Make sure beforehand that there's nothing you have to do, that you trust the people that you are with, and that you're in a safe and comfortable place. The feelings can be amazingly intense and pleasurable. You may find yourself laughing at the most insane things or grinning from ear to ear. Or, you might find yourself simply enjoying the subtlest of feelings or thoughts in a quiet and completely fulfilling way.

If challenging feelings come up, and if you have the space for it–and you can see and think straight enough for it in the moment–I'd recommend a bit of journaling. If the trip is still too intense for that, allow yourself some reflective time or lay back and journey. Let it come; let yourself feel whatever it has to show you, and let the decisions about what to do about these feelings come later. During the comedown, you can decide how you would like to approach life based on the emotions you have experienced.

MENTAL PSYCHEDELIC EFFECTS

The mental effects are some of the most profound of the trip, though in other ways than the emotional. As mentioned above, the psychedelic experience can lead to a dissolution of the ego. But what does that really mean?

The ego is our story about who we are. About what we like. How the world works for us. What is possible. What is *not* possible. What we want to do, and what we don't want to do. Basically, our ego is the whole framework of our experience. And this is what the psychedelic experience can dissolve.

Suddenly, you're back to basics. Back to being a center-point of experience surrounded by a field of stimuli. And the meaning that you apply to this field of stimuli is much more flexible than under normal circumstances. It's much easier to be abstract, as the familiar reference points have been stripped away. It's also easier to come up with way-out-there connections, which should probably be re-examined under less altered circumstances. They may provide great insight. Or they may be leading you way out on a limb. Either way, it's best to re-evaluate these insights when you can come from a more grounded space.

It's likely that, during your psilocybin experience, you come to realizations that are impossible to express, beautiful, blinding points of awareness that can change everything–only to have them fade with the trip. It's equally likely for these points of realization to stay with you and change your entire approach to life. Most of the time, for the better. The key is to stay grounded. If you have to write a book for people to read before they can understand your perspective, it's possible that your mental journey has been taken further than it needs to go. That's all up to you, and entirely subjective.

Once again, I'd recommend a bit of journaling. You may strike some absolute gold when in the journey, and you may come upon some things that you simply can't understand from a normal perspective. Sometimes, it will be both at once.

From a biological point of view, the psychedelic experience allows more parts of your brain to communicate with one another. This means, potentially, that you will be able to draw in aspects of cognition and understanding which are difficult to access under normal conditions. It may also mean that the thinking process is a bit scrambled and connections are being made that have little validity. In all likelihood, a little of both is occurring. Save the pieces of gold and see if you can integrate them into your normal waking understanding. If you've never tripped before, you might think this an easy process. If you have, then you know it's as simple as preserving that beautiful insight you got while dreaming. Not impossible, but not possible every time.

One of the most powerful ways that the mental aspect of the trip can be used is to make your ego fluid and recrystallize it in a different form. To do this constructively first requires an appropriate set and setting. These will be discussed further in the text. Second, you will want to listen to the powerful emotions or lessons that come up. These provide guidance.

They are the "loose ends" that are suppressed under normal circumstances. Third, figure out how you would like to change your approach to life, people, and experience based upon what has been revealed to you in the journey. This is for the comedown phase. Finally, when integrating these lessons into your life, do so with concrete action. This will make the trip a transformative experience rather than just a powerful memory.

CHAPTER 4. PSILOCYBIN MUSHROOMS AND SAFE USE

SET

SETTING

SUBSTANCE

SITTER

SESSION

STAGE 1: INGESTING THE PSYCHEDELIC

STAGE 2: INITIAL ONSET

STAGE 3: OPENING AND LETTING GO

STAGE 4: PLATEAU

STAGE 5: GENTLE GLIDE

STAGE 6: END OF THE FORMAL SESSION

FINAL NOTES ABOUT SESSION

SITUATION

Most people who have done a bit of study into the psychedelic experience will have encountered two of the conditions for safe use: set and setting. Set refers to the mindset you hold when entering and navigating the trip. Setting addresses the physical location in which you enter the psychedelic experience. However, there are four other conditions that are of equal importance. These are substance, sitter, session, and situation. Taken together, they form the six S's which help to prime an individual to use the trip constructively.

In this chapter, I'll go through all of these conditions in detail, explaining how you can approach the situation to provide the best possible experience. These conditions are important to consider whether you enter into a psychedelic experience with the aid of psilocybin or any other entheogens. In fact, the substance itself is one of the six S's, so I'll provide the details of this condition with psilocybin mushrooms in mind.

SET

As mentioned above, "set" refers to mindset. When ingesting psilocybin or any other hallucinogen, the thoughts and emotions you carry into the trip will be amplified. Because of this, preparation is extremely important. This holds true whether you are a novice or you have tripped thousands of times. The main difference between an inexperienced individual and an experienced one is that experience will tend to make the preparation phase reflexive. Your mental preparation will have a huge impact on your personal experience during the trip.

One thing that is important to remember is that the preparation phase is equally important for both the voyager and the guide. It is not a small thing to act as a guide or sitter for an individual experiencing a trip, especially if they are tripping for the first time or are relatively inexperienced. If you are the guide, then the voyager is placing a huge amount of trust in you. They are relying upon you to provide an anchor when feelings and thoughts become intense. More than that, they are placing themselves in one of the most psychologically vulnerable states a human being can experience.

During the trip, it is important for the guide to remain watchful while giving the voyager space to have their experience. Pay attention to where they go, to how they are feeling, but do not interfere unless necessary. The voyager is the most important thing during the trip. Make sure there is nothing else you have to do, and that you can be there for them fully during the experience. If they become lost and encounter difficulty, it is your responsibility to call them back to presence with calm and gentleness. Facilitating a trip is an art, and should only be done by those who have extensive tripping experience.

For the voyager, remember that the trip is not a recreational experience. It is a transformative and healing journey, one in which your mind and being are opened to new aspects of experience. The trip offers a powerful opportunity to heal buried trauma, to learn new things, and to reshape the way you approach the world. You can use this time to heal old wounds, let go of unhealthy habits, or tap into deep and profound levels of insight. You can frame the experience to help you work through any challenges you may be facing in life. However, in order to do this, you must face the trip as a sacred experience rather than as a simple drug trip.

With this in mind, try to schedule enough time to truly honor the experience. One of the best approaches is to give yourself three days. The first day is for preparation and clarification. The second is for the psilocybin experience. The third is for grounding and the integration of what you have learned and the experiences you have had. You may also wish to use the third day to record any insights you have received or discoveries you have made.

During the first day, try to remain calm and unhurried. It's best if you can wrap up any loose ends before this day, but if there is anything which needs to be addressed, take care of it so there's nothing weighing on your mind. It's best if you are able to spend some of the day in nature. Try to set aside a bit of time for self-reflection.

If you are inexperienced, it is especially helpful to do a bit of focused journaling on the first day. Ask yourself a few questions: Do you have any preconceptions regarding the psilocybin experience? Do you have any expectations from the trip? Is there anything you hope to learn from the trip? To experience? To understand? To resolve? Do you have any particular goals? Psychological? Social? Spiritual?

As your guide should be experienced with psychedelics, they will be able to address any concerns you might have and help you approach the trip from a calm and collected place. Your guide should also be able to answer any questions you have regarding the experience, to the extent that questions can be answered. Remember that the trip is a personal experience, and there is no way to know where you will take it–or it will take you–before you begin.

A final note regarding set: while it is helpful to clarify your expectations and intentions, it is equally important to surrender them prior to the trip. Trips don't follow our expectations. Whatever you have to address will come up during your experience. It may be what you intend, or it may be what really needs attention regardless of your intentions. Furthermore, if you have done a great deal of study prior to the trip, you may have high expectations of what the experience will bring you. Remember that what we get hardly ever looks the way we expect it to. Just allow it to be, and it will bring you where you need to go.

SETTING

Setting relates to your external environment and surroundings. During a psilocybin experience, you will be far more sensitive to sights, sounds, emotions, and thoughts than you might normally be. It is important to set the space for your session and choose the environment wisely. As mentioned above, it is unwise for an inexperienced person to go into an uncontrolled setting during their first trip. That means that clubs and parties aren't great settings for your first psychedelic experience. You'll want to choose a place where you can be you, no matter what comes up, and where you can behave however you wish without being judged or needing to maintain an image.

If you choose to trip indoors, then you will want the room to be uncluttered and comfortable. You will also want a bed or couch available so that you can lie down if the mood strikes you. Make sure that you have soft pillows and blankets. You'll also want access to a toilet and plenty of water. Another good tip is to have a stereo or other sound system ready to go with smooth, mellow music. Basically, you want to prepare the space so that everything you might want is easily accessible. The space should be arranged so that it brings you a sense of peace.

The second option is to trip in an outdoor setting. If you choose to go this route, you'll want a familiar place where you are comfortable and where you can do what you want without observation or censorship. The outdoor experience is more extroverted and will likely bring a strong sense of connection with nature. Even when tripping outdoors, though, you will want to make sure you can lie down comfortably. It's also an excellent idea to bring along a blanket and music.

You may wish to alternate between outside and inside. If this is the case, then it's best to find an easily accessible outdoor space. You won't want to be driving from one place to the next. The psychedelic experience is often more intense when internalized, when in an indoor space. Conversely, while outside, the senses are pulled outward into nature. You may wish to begin inside and go outside to explore nature when things get intense, or start outside and let things build slowly before taking things indoors and allowing the trip to rise to a strong peak. While in the experience, you will often feel powerful and unexpected impulses. It's best to listen to them, so long as you can do so safely.

The sensory enhancement of the psilocybin experience makes music extremely enjoyable and powerful. In fact, most tribal cultures that employ entheogens in their spiritual ceremonies also include music as an essential element of the process. Music serves as a sensory guide to lead the consciousness from one level of awareness to another. It also provides a stream of sensory stimuli, which can focus and direct the consciousness. In the psychedelic experience, music is extremely effective in eliciting emotions and guiding awareness down certain channels. It can provide the voyager with a feeling of safety and a sense of nonverbal support during their experience.

One thing that you may want to keep in mind is that your tastes may change under the influence of psilocybin and other psychedelics. If you normally enjoy loud, wild music, you may find that this music is grating and uncomfortable. Music with words may be distracting, especially once the experience peaks. You may wish to opt for soft, instrumental pieces that provide a smooth feeling. Tribal rhythms, chanting, and drumming may also be extremely pleasurable. You will actually feel the music as it carries you through the melody. The feeling of the music will intensify when you close your eyes, use an eyeshade, or listen to it in the dark.

You may also wish to make sure that you have access to drawing or writing materials. When the trip is extremely intense, these may lay by the wayside, but in the come up and come down, they can be beautiful allies. The same goes for musical instruments if you play them regularly. You may not want them at all, but it's nice to have them at hand if the feeling strikes.

The main thing is that you want to set things up so that you don't have to go anywhere or do anything complex. I've even found times where blankets were ridiculously complex in the thick of the trip, believe it or not. So, the simpler, the better.

SUBSTANCE

The third "S" is related to substance, but really, a better word for it is dosage. Regardless of the psychedelic substance you take, the dosage has a powerful influence on the experience. One of the challenges with psilocybin mushrooms is that the level of psilocybin varies from one strain to the next and from one mushroom to the next within a single strain, depending on growing conditions and age. There is less variation in cultivated mushrooms than in those grown in the wild.

There is a relationship between potency, dosage and the level of intensity that you will experience. A simple table looks at this relationship just for P.cubensis, which has an average potency of 0.63% of psilocybin.

Intensity	Avg. Wt. (dried)	Avg. Wt. (fresh)
Threshold	0.25g	2.5g
Light	0.25-1g	2.5-10g
Medium	1-2.5g	10-25g
Strong	2.5-5g	25-50g
"Heroic"	Above 5g	Above 50g

The relationship between dosage and intensity of experience - P.cubensis

As you can see, the percentage of active ingredients in dried mushrooms is about 10 times as high as in fresh mushrooms.

The threshold amount for psychedelics is the minimum amount needed to feel an alteration in consciousness. For dried Psilocybe cubensis, the threshold amount for the average person is 0.25g. A voyager will typically experience a light trip after ingesting between 0.25g and 1g. Medium trips often result from the ingestion of between 1g and 2.5g. A strong dose for the average person is considered between 2.5g and 5g. Anything over 5g is considered a "heroic" dose, meaning that this dose can be expected to provide an extremely powerful alteration in consciousness.

For fresh mushrooms you can consider the threshold amount of fresh Psilocybe cubensis mushrooms to be 2.5g. A light dose is between 2.5g and 10g. A medium dose is between 10g and 25g. A strong dose is between 25g and 50g. A "heroic" dose of fresh mushrooms is considered to be anything over 50g.

However, if you are using anything other than cubes, the following information on potency will be helpful.

SPECIES	% PSILOCYBIN	% PSILOCIN	% BAEOCYSTIN
P. azurescens	1.78	.38	.35
P. bohemica	1.34	.11	.02
P. semilanceata	.98	.02	.36
P. baeocystis	.85	.59	.10
P. cyanescens	.85	.36	.03
P. tampanensis	.68	.32	n/a
P. cubensis	.63	.60	.025
P. weilii	.61	.27	.05
P. hoogshagenii	.60	.10	n/a
P. stuntzii	.36	.12	.02
P. cyanofibrillosa	.21	.04	n/a
P. liniformans	.16	n/d	.005

The psilometric scale of comparative potency of selected Psilocybe mushrooms[1]

There is a significant difference in the potency of different species, ranging from 1.78% for *P. azurescens* to 0.16 for *P liniformans*. *P. cubensis* is in the mid-range at 0.63%. There have also been some findings that *Cyanescens* is in fact

[1] https://erowid.org/plants/mushrooms/mushrooms_info4.shtml (accessed Jan 23, 2019)

much more potent than indicated in this table and can go as high as 1.96%, making it even more potent than *P. azurescens*. So please be careful if you use it.

Working from this potency list, we can start to work out what the dosage should be. A rule of thumb is to start with less rather than more, especially if it is the first time you are using a species. Your metabolism is different to other people and you will need to work out how you react and what your dose tolerance is. Remember too that your body adjusts to mushrooms and they become less effective if you take them at short intervals, even if you try to take more to counteract this. So, it is better to find the right dosage for one time and then wait for about a month before using them again.

Here are some recommended dosages for different species.

#	Species	Common names	Dosage
1	P. azurescens	Blue Angels Blue Runners Indigo Psilocybe" Flying Saucer Mushroom Astoriensis	Most potent of the P's with psilocybin levels of 1,78%. Avoid eating more than an eighth of one mushroom at first. Nearly three times as potent as cubensis
2	P. bohemica	Now usually known as P. serbica. Previously also called P. arcana and P. moravica.	Considered to be similar to P. cyanescens, and dosage also probably similar.
3	P. semilanceata	Liberty Cap Witches Hat	20-40 fresh specimens or 1-2g dried. First timers should limit their first try to 25 fresh specimens maximum. As a guide, if you have bulk amounts: there are 30-40 doses in 500g fresh or 30g dried.
4	P. baeocystis	Baeos Knobby Tops Blue Bells	Strong dose is 1-3 fresh or 1g dry. Potency is reduced by half with drying

#	Species	Common names	Dosage
5	P. cyanescens	Cyans Blue Halos Wavy-Capped Psilocybe Blue meanies	1 large or 2-3 small specimens. Half a gram, dried (Some sources say that Psilocybin content varies from 0.66% - 1.96%, and believe that it is the most potent of the genus).
6	P. tampanensis*	This species develops sclerotia – truffles.	From truffles: 4–5g for a light trip. 5 9g for a medium trip. 10–15 g for a strong trip.
7	P. cubensis	Golden Tops Cubies San Isidro Hongos Kentesh Also known as cubes or shrooms	An ounce of fresh flesh. This can be 2 or 40 mushrooms, depending on size. Average recreational dose is 1g dried or 5g for heroic intensity.
9	P. hoogshagenii		1g dried
10	P. stuntzii	Blue Ringers Stuntz's Blue Legs Stuntz's Psilocybe	8g fresh or 20-30 specimens. 1-3g dried.
11	P. cyanofibrillosa	Rhododendron Psilocybe Blue-Haire Psilocybe	2-5 small or 1 large fresh specimens. Consuming dried not recommended as this species loses 70% potency during dehydration.
12	P. liniformans		Similar to cyanofibrillosa.
13	P.mexicana*	Flesh of the gods	5g for a light trip, 10g for a medium, 15 g for a strong trip This is a truffle (sclerotia).
14	P. atlantis*	Rare. Close relative to P. Mexicana Fruits of delight	4–5g for a light trip. 15 g for a strong trip. This is a truffle (sclerotia).
15	P. pelliculosa		This is a relatively weak mushroom. 20-50g fresh or 2-5g dried.
16	P. sylvatica		20-40g fresh or 2-4g dried.
17	P. antioquiensis		15-20 fresh or 1-2g dried.
18	P. samuiensis	Mainly from Thailand	15–20 fresh.

*Can also be consumed in truffle form.

Recommended dosages for psilocybin species

To be noted is that some of these species develop the normal mushroom fruiting bodies above ground, and also so-called sclerotia (commonly known as "magic truffles") below ground. They have the same active compounds, but it is not certain whether they produce exactly the same experience.

This table has been organized from strongest potency to lowest. The first two have extremely high potency and should be handled with caution. Numbers 3 to 5, potency is high–handle with respect!

If we go back to the P. cubensis table, the levels of intensity have been given for each dose. You might want to keep a similar table to record the dosages for other species that you try.

At threshold doses, a voyager can expect colors to seem somewhat brighter and mood to be elevated. Music will seem "wider," and the voyager may experience some short-term memory anomalies. The threshold experience leaves the journeyer feeling slightly stoned during the course of the trip.

At light doses, the voyager can expect a significant brightening of colors as well as visual effects like trails, halos, and perceived movement of stationary objects. When the eyes are closed, the voyager may experience dimensional patterns. Creativity is vastly increased and memory alterations become more profound. The voyager may also experience confused or distractive thought patterns and reminiscent thoughts may begin to arise.

Medium dosages will result in obvious visuals. Things will tend to look curved and warped. The voyager will see kaleidoscopic patterns on viewed objects such as walls and faces. At this dosage, the voyager will experience mild hallucinations such as "mother of pearl" surfaces and flowing rivers within wood grains. Low levels of synesthesia will begin to occur. Sights and sounds can be felt, etc. When the eyes are closed, the visuals will tend to take on a three-dimensional quality. At a medium dose, the voyager's sense of time will stretch and distort, giving them a sense that the moment is lasting forever.

At high doses, things start to get interesting. The hallucinations become very strong and the voyager may see objects melting or morphing into other objects. It is at this point that the ego begins to dissolve or split. With a splitting of the ego, the voyager may experience internal conversations, or they may be externalized as perceived elements of experience begin talking to them. They may also begin to feel contradictory things at the same time. At this point, both time and reality tend to lose meaning.

Synesthesia becomes pronounced, and the voyager may experience both ESP-type experiences and out-of-body phenomena. However, by this point, it is almost impossible to describe the personal experience, as it moves into a point beyond words. The trip, when experienced, may feel completely dissimilar to what is described, because it is moving beyond what is impossible to describe.

At heroic doses, sensory experiences become so profoundly altered that they bear little similarity to normal reality. The ego is entirely dissolved, and the voyager may tend to merge with other objects, space, and the universe itself. The experience itself cannot be described. Perceptual and thought patterns are altered so profoundly that they pick up on things beyond anything that can be put into words or sensible concepts.

For experienced trippers, the heroic dose can be used to engage with reality in truly transcendent ways. This dose is not recommended for those with little experience, as it may simply be too intense. Go this far and you are entering freak-out level. It can still be therapeutic, as the complete dissolution of the ego can allow a constructive shift in approach to life and others. This being said, most often a high dose will be sufficient for most journeying intents, and medium doses will work for emotional therapy. However, it can be extremely transformative for an individual to experience a heroic dose at least once in their tripping experience. A trip this intense is like a complete death of the ego, and after you experience that, there's little left to fear.

SITTER

The sitter or guide is extremely important for first-time users. In some instances, the guide is termed a facilitator. The responsibility of the facilitator is to create a healthy, calm space for the voyager. As mentioned above, this facilitator should have extensive experience with hallucinogens. They need to understand where the voyager will be likely to go during the trip and meet them there when necessary. Furthermore, it is not sufficient for the guide to merely have experience with psilocybin themselves. Guides for first-time users should be experienced in guiding others through the trip.

Some suggest that the guide or facilitator should be sober throughout the experience. This is a valid perspective; however, another alternative is to microdose through the experience. When the guide microdoses, they are able to stay in the same mental vibration as the voyager. However, the guide must be fully aware of how they will respond to psilocybin so that they can make sure that they will be in the appropriate place for the voyager.

During the trip, the guide acts as an anchor for the voyager. They will take care of all the little details that come up, such as the need for water, food, music, and, if necessary, transportation. (If the guide is responsible for transportation by vehicle, complete sobriety is recommended.)

The voyager is likely to experience moments of disorientation. The guide should act as a stable point during these disoriented times. In some instances, the voyager will become lost in their own thoughts and feelings. The guide should stay sufficiently aware of these mental movements that they know when it is right to leave the voyager to their journey, and when it is right to softly and gently bring them back to the present. This is something that cannot be explained. As mentioned above, it's an art and an extremely important one. Nothing more than extensive experience can prepare an individual to sit vigil for a voyager.

In no circumstance should an inexperienced person sit without a guide. However, this being said, there are some people who are naturally disposed to the psychedelic experience and others who find it more difficult to navigate a trip. If you are an individual who is naturally disposed to the psychedelic experience, then you may not need a guide. The problem is that there is no way to know this until you have tripped several times yourself.

The key is to stay calm, breathe, and relax. Remember that the experience will end in its own time and that you will be completely fine. When things get really challenging, all you have to do is wait it out. And, most of all **Don't Panic!** If you can remember that in the trip, then everything will work out fine. But it can be more difficult to keep these things in mind while tripping than you might expect. So, *please* find someone who can guide you through your experience before choosing to take a psychedelic substance for the first time.

At the very least, if an experienced person is unavailable, find a trusted friend who can watch out for you as you trip. Also, make sure that you carefully attend to set, setting, substance, session, and situation.

SESSION

The fifth S, Session, is associated with the time taken for the journey and the stages involved. Each trip involves a series of six stages. These six stages are: ingesting the psychedelic, the initial onset, opening up and letting go, the plateau, the gentle glide, and the end of the formal session.

Understanding the stages of the trip can be extremely helpful for first-time users, both in knowing what to expect and in being able to navigate the trip as they experience it. Knowing the stages can give a novice an understanding of the hour-by-hour progression of the session. The specific experience will differ from person to person and trip to trip, however, the stages remain the same. Here is a description of each stage:

STAGE 1: INGESTING THE PSYCHEDELIC

With regard to external experience, Stage 1 is pretty self-explanatory. With psilocybin mushrooms, this is the time that you eat the mushrooms or drink the mushroom tea. However, there are a few tips that will help you to navigate the experience from here on in.

The first tip is to check the clock when ingesting the 'shrooms. As soon as the psilocybin begins to kick in, your time sense will begin to become distorted. So, you'll want to have a solid clock-check before things get going. Often, you'll begin to feel the effects within about 20 minutes to a half hour. In some instances, it may take up to one hour. So, don't worry if it takes a little while to kick in. It will happen, so long as you have taken the threshold amount for your personal body chemistry. And when you're inexperienced, it's better to err on the side of caution than to take more because you have become impatient.

The second invaluable tip for this stage is to RELAX. When you ingest the mushroom, or right before you do so, take a breath and let it out all the way. If you meditate, then now's the time to enter the meditative state. Let go of everything, and let this be the state from which you enter the trip. This will pay off more than you may imagine over the next several hours.

If you are a first-time user and still have anxiety about the trip, you may wish to speak to your guide for last-minute reassurances. However, at this point, it's best if you have those out of the way. You've bought the ticket. You're taking the ride. All you can do is just let go and let the trip take you where it wants to take you.

STAGE 2: INITIAL ONSET

As you begin to feel the effects, you may wish to lie down. Or not. If you're outside, the effects can be amazing if you are walking around. There are no set rules. Just let the energy take you where it wants to take you. Essentially, the energy will rise up and your senses will begin to become crisper. Your sense of reality and time may begin to waver as the first effects of psilocybin begin to hit. Once again, breathe, meditate (if you're the type of person that meditates), and make sure that you're near where you want to be when it really hits.

The breath is the key. Breath keeps us in tune with our bodies and with the moment. It is like the steady beat of a drum that can keep us focused and in rhythm. Your breath is your best friend, all the way through the trip. Use it to find a path to relaxation. Remember, relaxing and surrendering will make the trip the best experience it can be.

During this time, you will begin to feel slightly inebriated. You may wish to start the music at this point, if you have chosen to include it in your experience, and if it is available. Observe all five senses. Tune in to what your body is experiencing right now. As the rushes of different impressions, thoughts, and images come in, allow them to wash over you. See them as an observer, watching everything without trying to control anything.

STAGE 3: OPENING AND LETTING GO

The initial build-up will lead to the peak, the point of opening up and letting go. This is the point where the trip peaks and you first begin feeling the full effects. Senses are heightened, time begins to become ever more slippery, and interesting thoughts come in. At this point, it's important to remind yourself to let go of any expectations. What will happen, will happen. Just let it be.

You don't have to make any decisions during the peak. You don't have anything to do other than to experience what the trip brings to you. This stage usually lasts about two to three hours, and it is the time that brings you fully into the consciousness of the trip. Thoughts and emotions are enhanced. Your sight begins to shift and flow. Your thoughts begin to depart from their typical path, and anything that is shown to you is part of this journey, whether pleasant or unpleasant. Try to simply allow whatever comes in.

The more you are able to fully let go of control, the more you allow yourself to move into the heart of the experience. At this time, you may experience unusual thoughts or feelings. Some of them may be old baggage coming up to be seen. Other feelings may simply be unusual and without context, but they are all part of the journey. You may feel yourself an alien or outsider. Or, you may feel like you're actually seeing what's around you for the first time ever. Embrace whatever feeling you experience. If you are having a hard time with it, turn to your guide. They'll help you along the way.

STAGE 4: PLATEAU

After about two to three hours have passed, you've stepped fully into the trip. The new feelings that came in over the last few hours have normalized, and this is your new state of being.

Remember, you will come down. You'll be normal eventually. But, this time is valuable. Thoughts about your life will continue to roll through, and now new insights will accompany them. Reality as you know it may seem inaccessible, and you will feel the trip strongly. However, this is the time that can teach you the most.

You can check in with your guide if you need to, but often, all you'll need is a little time to put things into perspective. As you do, you will continue to make new discoveries about yourself. You will feel into what you have done before and whether it is right for you or wrong for you, and you will get a clear notion of what you should do in your movement forward.

The plateau will last from one to two hours, though it may feel like a lifetime or three. Whatever lessons you receive in this time, respect them. See them for the blessings that they are, pleasant or not. These messages tell you how you truly want to move forward. In the process of receiving these aspects of yourself, do what you like. Listen to music. Journal. Play an instrument. Walk in nature. Do whatever you feel like doing. There's no wrong or right way to experience this phase of the trip. Do whatever you feel is right.

STAGE 5: GENTLE GLIDE

During the plateau stage, you will have become acclimatized to the trip. The next stage is when the comedown begins. You can think of it as a gentle glide back to a more normal frame of mind, a slow return to reality. Rational thought starts to come back into focus and the inebriation begins to fade.

During the comedown period, your insights are still fresh, but you are better able to bring these insights into connection with normal waking consciousness. This is a time when journaling can be extremely helpful. By writing or reviewing your experience, you take steps towards integrating what you have learned into life. This is also helpful because the insights may tend to fade as rational thought reasserts itself. By preserving these thoughts in a journal, you'll have better access to them at later times.

Sometimes, instead of doing personal work and reviewing the experience, you'll just want to enjoy the comedown and soak everything in. This is a beautiful time for walking in nature or curling up with a nice cup of coffee or tea. It can also be beautiful to lay back with a warm blanket and listen to music as you ease into sleepy, quiet energy. If you choose to experience nature in this time, it can leave you with a deep sense of presence and a vibrant aliveness, almost a sense of oneness and wonder with everything you see and feel.

STAGE 6: END OF THE FORMAL SESSION

At this point, you have come down, for the most part, but you are left with new perspectives and a general sense of openness. If the trip has been particularly intense, you may feel intense gratitude to finally be "normal" again, or at least more normal that you were a few short hours before. The trip will often highlight people and connections in your life that you truly value, so during this period, you may feel greater love and acceptance for the people in your life. In general, you may feel a strong sense of the beauty and preciousness of every aspect of life.

As with the comedown period, this is an excellent time to record your thoughts. If the trip has shown you things that you would like to approach differently, then this is an excellent time to make decisions about how you would like to do so. Any aspects of life that have been up for review or simply shown to you might bear a few words or thoughts. The trip involves a profound reorganization of neural patterns, and these patterns will provide new perspectives and realizations that remain with you even as your brain activity returns completely to normal. Right after the experience has ended you are best able to record or verbalize these perspectives and insights.

FINAL NOTES ABOUT SESSION

Though these stages described above give a fair indication of the general course of experience, every single trip is different. Each person's experience is different. There is no way to accurately generalize the situation. Your experience will be absolutely unique, each and every time you enter into a psychedelic journey.

The important thing here is not to be lulled into a false sense of confidence regarding what you will experience. Yes, it can help to understand the stages so that you can navigate them more effectively. But, in the moment, the trip is something so alive and present that all anyone can do is embrace the experience and dance with it.

SITUATION

The final S, Situation, refers to the time after the trip. That means the days, weeks, and months after your experience. No part of life can be cut off and perceived in isolation. Every moment in our lives is connected to every other. This means that what the trip has offered you really begins, in a practical sense, in the period that follows. This is when you can bring this new awareness into your decision-making process on a day-to-day basis.

Many who journey regularly describe this as the "unpacking" process. So much comes through so quickly during the trip that it may take some time to unpack all of the lessons and insights. To facilitate the unpacking process, a period of personal review is advisable. During this personal review, you may wish to ask yourself some questions:

- Have you had any revelations regarding thought processes or perspectives, daily habits or routines?
- Are there people in your life that you would like to connect with more closely, or that you would like to show their value to you through your actions?
- Are there people that should be left behind so that you can continue to grow and thrive?
- Are there any goals you would like to move towards? Endeavors that you would like to dedicate your energy to?

These are just a few guiding questions. You may find that others pop up for you based on what you have experienced. When making any shifts, remember to be gentle with yourself. It can take some time to reprogram your approach to life. Slow and steady makes it solid and sustainable.

The psychedelic experience can be profound, and most will want to discuss it with others. But remember that it is unique and personal. Others who have not tripped may be unable to understand what you share, especially on the feeling level. So, don't be discouraged if it is challenging to express why you are making these shifts. What you have experienced is valid because *you have experienced it.* You don't need any external validation for your insights.

Finally, depending on your experience, you may either feel that you would never like to try psilocybin again, or you may wish to relive the experience. If you do wish to experience it again, it is often best to have some time between trips. This will help each experience to be as profound as possible. It will also give you some time to unpack each journey before you go on the next. As with everything else, this is a profoundly personal choice, with no right or wrong answers. Feel into it.

Chapter 5. Psilocybin Mushrooms: Therapeutic Use, Personal Growth, and Microdosing

Therapeutic Use

Personal Growth

Microdosing

Chapter 5. Psilocybin Mushrooms: Therapeutic Use, Personal Growth, and Microdosing

As this book is primarily focused on safe use and cultivation, the subjects of therapeutic use and microdosing will be discussed only briefly. The use of psychedelics for personal growth is discussed only tangentially as well. Each of these subjects is extensive enough to fill a volume of their own. If you'd like to explore the subject deeper, I recommend looking into some of my other books or the works of many other experienced psychonauts.

Therapeutic Use

In the material above, I've offered some details as to how psilocybin and psychedelics, in general, can be used therapeutically. Testing of psilocybin by the medical community is still in its infancy, as laws have only begun to allow limited investigation within the last decade. The medical community is currently exploring its medical uses for a number of conditions. These include depression, addiction, PTSD, cluster headaches and migraines, OCD, and mood and anxiety disorders. Results thus far have been promising in each of these areas.

It's worth mentioning that initial results suggest psilocybin is far more effective in the treatment of depression than anything currently accepted for medical use. Results come more quickly and tend to be longer lasting than other drugs on the market. In addition, unlike these other drugs, patients using psilocybin for treatment of depression do not need to be continuously medicated for the treatment to be effective. In addition, initial research into the use of psilocybin treatment for addiction is more promising by far than any form of treatment thus far discovered.

Psilocybin also has great potential for emotional healing. PTSD and mood and anxiety disorder are just a few of the conditions that have been responsive to psilocybin therapy. Similar studies have shown that psilocybin has been effective at significantly reducing the emotional pain associated with social rejection.

There is no doubt that further studies will show the profound benefits of psilocybin and other psychedelics for treating trauma and all forms of emotional healing. Given the deep impact of emotion on every aspect of our lives, this suggests that psychedelics may be the single most powerful healing tool available to us.

It's noteworthy that a new research division has recently been set up and funded in the Psychiatric Department of the John Hopkins Hospital in the USA, specifically to look at the potential therapeutic effects of psychedelics–and especially psilocybin mushrooms and cannabis.

In the meantime, some relatively recent research undertaken by Dr Griffiths et al from John Hopkins University[2], is interesting and may provide some guidelines about the

---

[2] Griffiths RR, Richards WA, McCann U, Jesse R., *Psilocybin can occasion mystical-type experiences having substantial and sustained personal meaning and spiritual significance.*/https://www.ncbi.nlm.nih.gov/pubmed/16826400 (accessed September 23, 2019)

dosages you choose for yourself. This research helps to explain why, although it is impossible to overdose on mushrooms from a toxicity point of view and they are not addictive, it is necessary to exercise caution because of the intensity of the effects you may experience.

Griffiths et al were looking at possible therapeutic uses for psilocybin, especially for depression and PTSD, in view of its reported long-term positive effects.

They administered varying strengths of psilocybin to 30 volunteers in one study and followed it up with a similar study with 18 volunteers a few years later. They used dosages of 5, 10, 20 and 30mg psilocybin per 70kg body weight of the volunteer, administered either in increasing or decreasing dosages, and at a rate of about once per month. On average this would translate to about 0.8g, 1.6g, 3.2g and 4.8g of dried P cubensis (and matches our description of light, medium, strong and "heroic" doses given earlier).

Some of their findings are useful:

- Doses of 20mg and 30mg produced a mystical experience for 72% of the group (this would be 3.2g and 4.8g in our P. cubensis calculation).
- One month and even 14 months after these higher dosages, participants rated the experience as having had noteworthy personal and spiritual significance. Up to 65% also reported sustained positive changes in attitude, mood and behavior after 30mg. The 20mg group had similar results, with 60% reporting sustained positive changes.
- Those who had had the ascending doses (i.e. starting low and getting stronger) reported the most positive

results. This result was not the same as other research, which suggests that an immediate very strong experience might have long-term positive therapeutic results.

- Those who monitored and recorded the sessions observed that most reactions increased with the increasing dosage[3]. For example, the chance of the participant crying increased with the dosage; arousal, distance from ordinary reality and happiness were highest at the 30mg dosage. However, interestingly, the highest level of peace/harmony was at the 20mg level.

Also, the researchers found that the 30mg dose gave rise to some unpleasant outcomes.

- It was the only level where monitors reported significant paranoid thinking.
- 86% of the participants experienced extreme fearfulness, and an average time of about 11 minutes of strong anxiety. By comparison, at the 20mg level, only 14% experienced extreme fearfulness, with only 2 minutes of extreme anxiety. At 10mg, there was no fearfulness and only 1 minute of strong anxiety.

So, it would seem wise to start with low dosages, with 20mg being the most effective and carefully consider your chances of having a bad trip if you try very high dosages.

3 Ronald F. Griffiths, Matthew W. Johnson, William A. Richards (2011): *Psilocybin occasioned mystical-type experiences: immediate and persisting dose-related effects*/https://www.ncbi.nlm.nih.gov/pmc/articles/PMC3308357/table/T1/ (accessed January 23, 2019)

PERSONAL GROWTH

While therapeutic benefits focus more on the use of psilocybin and other psychedelic compounds for healing, there may be huge benefits for healthy individuals as well. This is an exciting area of study, as it may provide a key for enhancing our capacity for healthy functioning on numerous levels. Therapeutic studies suggest that psilocybin can reduce the impact of negative states like social anxiety, distraction, and lack of motivation. At the same time, positive mental resources like creativity, cognitive function, and productivity have been enhanced through psilocybin use.

On a biological level, psilocybin has been shown to stimulate the growth of new brain cells and facilitate learning. Psilocin, the bioactive metabolite of psilocybin, stimulates the 5-HT2A serotonin receptors in the prefrontal cortex. This has two immediate biological effects. The first is an increased production of Brain Derived Neurotropic Factor (BDNF). Essentially, this stimulates the growth of neurons and neural connections and the activity of these neurons. At the same time, the brain produces more glutamate, a neurotransmitter responsible for learning, memory, and cognition.

With regard to global brain function, psilocybin dampens the activity of the Default Mode Network (DMN). This is a portion of the brain associated with a variety of mental activities including self-reflection, daydreaming, and thoughts of the past or future. When the activity of the DMN is dampened, it is easier for the brain to form new and different neural connections. This means learning new activities and information.

To put this into perspective, consider the act of concentration. Effective concentration requires present moment awareness. Thoughts of the past or future, excessive self-reflection, and daydreaming are dilutions of present moment awareness. They are processes that interfere with present moment awareness. Though these activities have their place, the DMN is often overactive, resulting in excessive self-analysis and counterproductive attention to memories or future possibilities. When the DMN has the volume turned down, the mind becomes more capable of focus and concentration, allowing us to be more productive and to learn new things more quickly and effectively.

Psilocybin also increases global neural function. In typical waking states, many parts of the brain operate more or less independently from one another. Psilocybin causes these parts of the brain to synchronize with one another, allowing more of the brain to operate as a whole rather than a collection of parts. The communication between these various regions is strengthened, and the linkages formed during the trip tend to persist even after the psychedelic experience has ended. In the process, the brain is "rebooted." It is reprogrammed and the neural activity is significantly reorganized.

Despite the advances of medical science, we still know very little about the brain compared to what is left to be discovered. Because of this, we cannot conclusively determine the impact of this reorganization. However, anecdotal evidence suggests that it is linked to greater empathy and compassion, higher levels of creativity and innovative thought, and the capacity to overcome fear-based blockages. These are just a few of the most profound and oft-cited results that have been described in the bulk of those who have used psilocybin.

As mentioned above, this is a subject that can be discussed extensively, and this book is dedicated more to safe use and psilocybin mushroom cultivation. However, before moving on, it is worthwhile to mention that moderate doses of psilocybin have been shown to shift the brain waves to the alpha rhythm, a state observed in both meditation and flow states. Higher doses have been linked to a dissolution of the ego, which, in turn, provides an opportunity to restructure our perception of ourselves and the world.

MICRODOSING

The use of psilocybin mushrooms and other psychedelics has historically been linked to powerful hallucinogenic experiences. Early research focused on the potential of psychedelics to induce mind-expanding spiritual experiences. These experiences were based on the capacity of large doses of psychedelic compounds to elicit profound changes in the perception of reality. However, in recent years, the practice of microdosing has been gaining attention. This involves the use of psychedelics to gain cognitive benefits without entering a full-blown trip.

Microdosing has, to some extent, increased the legitimacy of psychedelic use. One reason for this is that it is becoming popular among professionals in competitive industries such as those in Silicon Valley. By using a small amount of psilocybin or other psychedelic compounds, professionals are able to gain a competitive edge. Microdosing can help a user to increase creativity and productivity while reducing the effects of anxiety and depression. Furthermore, this is a practice that can have lasting benefits, even after the regimen has been completed.

Essentially, microdosing is exactly what it sounds like. When on a psilocybin mushroom microdosing regimen, a user will ingest a small, measured dose of psilocybin mushrooms. The effect is sub-perceptual, meaning that it is below the amount needed for a psychedelic experience. After ingestion, the user will then go about work or their regular routine just as they would under normal circumstances.

Though the psychological effects are subtle, the benefits can still be profound. They include improved energy levels, problem-solving capacity, and focus. Anecdotal evidence also suggests that microdosing is helpful for breaking unhealthy habits and cultivating healthy ones, increasing connection with nature, improving diet, and improving relationships.

The process of microdosing psilocybin mushrooms is fairly simple. You'll want to begin with a batch of dried mushrooms. Psilocybin content can vary widely from one strain to the next and even from one mushroom to another in the same strain. Because of this, it is helpful to powder the entire batch and mix it together to equalize the levels of psilocybin throughout the batch. If you begin with fresh mushrooms, it will be helpful to boil a measured amount into a tea. Measure the weight of fresh mushrooms that go into the tea, and divide the volume of the resulting tea so that each dosage corresponds to 1g of the starting mass.

For most people, 0.1g of dried mushrooms or 1g of fresh mushrooms will be sufficient to gain the benefits of microdosing. You can use this as a starter dose and then adjust levels as necessary. The goal is to have enough so that you experience very little change in mood, mindset, or disposition, while still feeling extremely subtle effects. You may also need to "recalibrate" with each new batch. This is why it is helpful to have one of the microdosing days on the weekend. It's best to have a bit of a buffer in case the new batch is more potent than the previous. Most of the time, it's not all that fun to be full-on tripping at work.

Another key to microdosing is to set up a schedule. Tolerance will increase quickly, so it is ideal to give yourself two days between each dose. If you want to set up a weekly schedule, for example, you may wish to dose on Wednesday and Sunday. By dosing twice per week, you will gain the full benefits of microdosing without increasing tolerance and needing to up the dosage. Alternately, you can simply dose every three days. For example, dose on day 1, take days 2 and 3 off, then dose again on day 4.

Because microdosing is intended as a means of improving performance and generally enhancing life experience, it will help to keep a journal of the effects. You may wish to note the amount that you have ingested and any specific results you have noticed throughout the course of the day or week. Since psilocybin causes a reorganization of neural activity, it is helpful to record any observations during the off-days as well.

Plus, it is helpful to have records when experimenting with different dosages. You may wish to assess results in areas like productivity, creativity, anxiety, and focus. Different dosages will have different effects on each area, so keeping records will help you to find your "sweet spot" for different activities and effects.

When first beginning your microdosing regimen, you may wish to do so on a day off work. This will help you to become accustomed to the feeling and to make sure the dosage is right for you. You may wish to follow the regimen for several weeks to a few months at first, and then take some time off. In the process, you will be able to observe and record the short-term and long-term effects, and see how these effects persist after the regimen has been completed.

Remember that the goal is to integrate these benefits into your daily life without becoming dependent upon the psychedelic substance. With infrequent use, psilocybin can be leveraged as an occasional advantage. In addition, you'll find that the benefits will remain with you even when you are not actively ingesting psilocybin mushrooms. They essentially lead the way to productive mental and emotional states. This can help you to access these states without assistance in the future.

Finally, despite the numerous benefits of microdosing and of psychedelics in general, it is important to remember that these substances are not magical cure-alls. They can facilitate personal growth and healing, but it requires intention and focus to leverage these effects for lasting benefits. Plus, the key to the benefits provided by psilocybin and other psychedelics is awareness. Essentially, mindfulness. Psilocybin helps us to actively engage with our mental state. By becoming more aware of our internal states, our emotions, our thoughts, and our focus, we constructively harness our attention and access more of our natural potential.

Chapter 6. Tips on Consumption

Ways to consume psilocybin

General tips on consumption

Chapter 6. Tips on Consumption

In the previous chapters, we focused on the experience you may have after ingesting magic mushrooms and on ensuring that you set yourself up for a safe and satisfying journey.

This chapter gives some practical tips about the best ways to actually consume the mushrooms. This may sound a lot more mundane, but it is important to ensure that you have the best experience.

A word of caution: If you are not going to cultivate your own psilocybins, be very careful of your sources. Aside from the danger of being sold a poisonous mushroom, there are imposters waiting to take your cash. According to the *European Monitoring Center for Drugs and Drug Addiction,* in a study of 886 samples sold as hallucinogenic mushrooms in the USA, only 28% were actually so. 35% of the sample proved to be normal edible mushrooms laced with drugs, mainly LSD or PCP (phencyclidine). The rest contained no drug at all.

Ways to consume psilocybin

Not surprisingly, there are many ways for you to ingest psilocybins, some safer than others. We would not recommend that you sniff, smoke or inject them. We also recommend that you <u>never</u> take magic mushrooms together with other drugs, especially alcohol and cannabis.

Rather, we would suggest that you take them orally. You can eat them raw or cooked with other foods to mask their bitter taste. They can be fresh or dried. Dried truffles can generally be substituted for dried mushrooms. You can mix them with something else–peanut butter and honey seem to be popular. Making teas is quick and easy. You can crush dried mushrooms or truffles and sprinkle them over foods or even make your own capsules for microdosing (remember to keep each capsule below 0.5g for this). You can find a list of recipes for your magic mushrooms in the Appendix.

GENERAL TIPS ON CONSUMPTION

Before we continue with recipes, there are a few general tips that you might want to keep in mind.

1. Nausea

Nausea may be the result of the taste or it can be a side effect of the drug. This can be accompanied by severe stomach cramps and even vomiting. To avoid this–and also to get a faster reaction–it's best to take the mushrooms on an empty stomach. Wait for about 2.5 hours after your last meal.

Making a tea and then straining out the solid bits also helps–nausea is caused by the indigestible chitin parts.

Magic mushrooms tend to suppress your appetite, but you might need to eat something during your trip. Fresh, healthy snacks are best–oranges, celery sticks, and non-fatty protein.

2. Water

Magic mushrooms are not toxic, but your body recognizes them as a chemical to be eliminated and will try to flush them from your system. If you are not drinking sufficient water, your body will draw it from other sources and you'll end up being dehydrated. Water will not alter the strength or the duration of the trip. Make sure you have placed about a liter of water near to you before you start–later on, even simple things like fetching a drink can become too complicated.

3. Chewing

Be sure to chew the mushrooms well as this starts the process of releasing the psychoactive compound. Otherwise, invest in a truffle grinder or coffee grinder and grind them to a paste. This may also reduce the time you have to taste them! Another tip is to add the mushrooms to your favorite smoothie. Pulse the blender a few times to mix in well.

4. Heat

Heat kills the active compound. Psilocybin breaks down at 200°C (about 390°F). So, it's better to add mushrooms to foods after they have been cooked–for example on top of an already cooked pizza or into a sauce or a pesto. Or cook for as short a time as possible and on low temperatures. Also, when you are making tea, allow the water to cool slightly after it has boiled before you add it to the mushrooms. When you are brewing the tea, make sure that the water is simmering but not boiling rapidly. However, as long as you are careful about the temperature, you can use pretty much any of your favorite recipes that have mushrooms in them and just substitute psilocybins.

5. Rehydrating dry mushrooms

It usually takes 20 to 30 minutes to rehydrate mushrooms. You want them to triple in size. The warmer the liquid the faster it will be–but not too hot, remember! So maybe use lukewarm liquid and wait for 30–40 minutes. Also, some of the active compounds will seep out into the liquid, so it's a good idea to use any liquid that remains in your recipe too.

6. Lemon and lime

We talk about psilocybin as the psychoactive compound in the mushroom, but it is actually a prodrug, meaning that it has to be converted into another drug–in this case psilocin–to be effective. Usually, this conversion happens through the action of stomach acids. But lemon or lime juice starts the process. When you add the juice to dried or fresh mushrooms, your stomach has less to do and the active compound is absorbed faster, so your trip starts faster and may end faster, but it will be more intense. You are also masking the taste, so the whole experience may be more pleasant.

In general, absorption is better from a liquid, so you can add your mushrooms to any juice. Open the bottle, drink a little, then add the crushed or dried mushrooms, replace the cap and shake well.

7. Chocolate

Chocolate with your mushrooms enhances their effect and can have a strong impact on the intensity of your experience. We recommend this only for experienced users. Be on the lookout for people selling "chocolate truffles"–or make your own.

8. Bad trips

Whether your bad trip is a result of too high a dose or from your own mindset before you started, you may need to lessen the effect. Vitamin C helps–take a high dose of about 1mg. If you don't have any, try a fruit juice. Sugary drinks also help.

9. Potency

Remember to check the potency and the recommended dosages before you just toss mushrooms into your food or drinks. There is some debate about whether mushroom truffles have the same level of potency as the mushroom fruits, but it is probably safest to assume that they are the same.

PART II
THE BASICS OF CULTIVATION

CHAPTER 7. COMMON PSILOCYBE SPECIES

COMMON SPECIES

PSILOCYBE AZURESCENS

PSILOCYBE BAEOCYSTIS

PSILOCYBE BOHEMICA

PSILOCYBE CUBENSIS

PSILOCYBE CYANESCENS

PSILOCYBE CYANOFIBRILLOSA

PSILOCYBE MEXICANA

PSILOCYBE PELLICULOSA

PSILOCYBE TAMPANENSIS

PSILOCYBE SEMILANCEATA

PSILOCYBE STUNTZII

PSILOCYBE SYLVATICA

PSILOCYBE WEILII

COMMON PSILOCYBE CHARACTERISTICS

UNDERSTANDING THE MUSHROOM

TRUFFLES VS MUSHROOMS

CHAPTER 7. COMMON PSILOCYBE SPECIES

Here comes some of the fun! These are some of the most common species of psilocybin mushroom, along with descriptions of their distinctive characteristics and the regions and environments where you are likely to find them.

You'll notice that many of the species described in this section are native to North America, specifically to the Pacific Northwest. Remember that the Western world only began to identify psilocybin species in earnest in the 1960s. Furthermore, though about 10,000 species of fungus have been identified in North America alone, mycologists estimate that this is only a third to a fifth of the existing North American species. There is no doubt that there are numerous unidentified species of magic mushroom in North America alone, and probably many times that number across the globe. So, consider these common in that they have been positively identified in terms of habitat, region, and use.

Please! Do not try to find or identify these species based upon the pictures and descriptions you see here, or any pictures and descriptions. It's easy to get fooled by look-alike species. And, according to a Croatian proverb, "All mushrooms are edible; but some only once."

Common Species

Psilocybe azurescens

Psilocybe azurescens is primarily native to western North America. It can be found most prolifically along the northern coast of Oregon. This mushroom prefers dune grasses and can be found most easily in the areas where the dune grasses meet the beach. It is closely associated with the Ammophila maritime species of dune grass.

Earthstongue/Shroomery.org

P. azurescens generates a very dense, tenacious, and extensive mycelial network. This mycelium often leeches surrounding wood, causing it to whiten. It fruits late in the season, often after the first frost. Fruiting bodies can be found in late December and early January. However, it is also extremely adaptable. It has been successfully cultivated outdoors in Ohio, Vermont, Wisconsin, and even New Mexico. Common names include "Blue Angels," "Blue Runners," "Indigo Psilocybe," "Flying Saucer Mushroom," and "Astoriensis"

PSILOCYBE BAEOCYSTIS

Psilocybe baeocystis is another species common to the northwest regions of North America. It can be found in British Columbia, Oregon, and Washington, as well as in surrounding coastal areas. This is a wood-loving mushroom, preferring lawns with high lignin content, wood mulch, or decaying conifer mulch. P. baeocystis can also be found growing on Douglas fir seed cones. P. baeocystis is another fungus with an extremely hardy mycelium, which means that it tolerates most conditions without the need to produce fruiting bodies.

Photo source: Trufflemagic.com

Because of this, the best times to search for it are during fall and early winter, when the mycelium is becoming stressed by the cold, but before it enters a hibernation period. It can occasionally be found in the spring or later, depending on climate conditions. Common names include "Baeos" and "Knobby Tops."

PSILOCYBE BOHEMICA

P.bohemica is believed to be the same species that is now more commonly called P. serbica. It was previously also identified and named as P. arcana and P. moravica.

It is quite rare, found mostly in Europe, and particularly in the Czech Republic. It is also not easy to cultivate. It is, however, one of the more potent species, with psilocybin levels as high as 1.34%.

Roberto/MushroomObserver.org

It is a wood-loving species and can be found in moist places on forest paths, roadside verges and along streams. It likes decaying deciduous and coniferous wood, plant residue, twigs and compost.

PSILOCYBE CUBENSIS

Psilocybin cubensis is the easiest psilocybin mushroom to grow indoors, making it the preferred strain for novice growers. In its natural habitat, it is a dung-loving mushroom. This means that it grows in cow fields, among other places. P. cubensis can also be found growing naturally in all continents except for Europe, Africa, and Antarctica.

uncredited/Shutterstock.com

Regions where P. cubensis can be commonly found include Mexico, Cuba, and Central America, northern South America, and the southeast U.S. It also grows naturally in India, Thailand, Vietnam, Cambodia, and the Queensland region of Australia. P. cubensis fruits most heavily in the two months prior to the hottest portion of the year. In the northern hemisphere, this is usually May and June, though one can find them into January under some conditions.

Though these are dung-loving mushrooms, they also grow on other substrates. Common names include "Golden Tops," "Cubies," "San Isidro," and "Hongos Kentesh."

PSILOCYBE CYANESCENS

P. cyanescens is native to the western coastal regions of North America, from California to the southern reaches of Alaska. It can also be found throughout the United Kingdom and much of Europe, including Spain, Germany, Italy, and Sweden. Common names include "Cyans," "Blue Halos," and "Wavy-Capped Psilocybe."

P. cyanescens loves humus and decaying wood. You can find them in wood chips, amongst leaves and twigs, in sawdust, and in woody debris or debris fields rich with rotting wood. They can also be found in the mixed woods at the edges of lawns, in rose gardens, and in the beds of heavily mulched rhododendrons.

PSILOCYBE CYANOFIBRILLOSA

Psilocybe cyanofibrillosa is another coastal Psilocybe species native to the Pacific Northwest. It can be found from British Columbia to Northern California. This species prefers to grow near bush lupines and along the flood plains of estuaries that empty into the Pacific Ocean. It also tends to grow in coastal rhododendron gardens and nurseries, which gives rise to one of its common names, the "Rhododendron Psilocybe." Its other common name is "Blue-Haired Psilocybe," due to the small hairs along the stem that turn bluish with age or when handled.

Photo source: Trufflemagic.com

PSILOCYBE MEXICANA

Psilocybe mexicana, one of the species used by the Mazatec Indians and by Maria Sabina in her veladas, has been found only in Mexico, Costa Rica, and Guatemala. It is most commonly found singularly or in groups in the grassy areas that border deciduous forests, or in clumps of moss along roadsides, trails, cornfields, or humid meadows. It is rare at lower elevations, but common at elevations from 300-550m (980-1800ft). This species most commonly fruits between May and October in these regions. It is also one of the best-known species to develop sclerotia, often called truffles.

AGCuesta/Shutterstock.com

PSILOCYBE PELLICULOSA

Psilocybe pelliculosa is another Psilocybe species indigenous to the Pacific Northwest and Northern California. This is a wood-loving species and grows in soils with high lignin content, as well as in mulch, along abandoned roads, on the decayed substratum of conifers, and along the paths of conifer forests.

dabjola/Shutterstock.com

PSILOCYBE TAMPANENSIS

Psilocybe tampanensis is an extremely rare fungus. It is one of the species of mushrooms that forms sclerotia or hard lumps in the mycelium–this is a food reserve to help the mycelium withstand drought and heat. It has been found only a few times in the wild near Florida in the USA. It gets its name from a sample collected by the mycologist Pollock from a sand dune in Tampa, Florida in 1977. Pollack was able to clone this sample and cultivate it in his laboratory. He was also able to induce the growth of sclerotia. From that laboratory, it has been taken around the world and has been successfully cultivated to produce consistent levels of potency. It is one of the most popular "magic truffles," especially in Europe.

PSILOCYBE SEMILANCEATA

Although the Psilocybe semilanceata is the species spread most widely across the globe, it is one of the most difficult to cultivate. It is indigenous to much of Europe, including France, Norway, Switzerland, and Holland. It can also be found in northern India, Chile, South Africa, and the South Island of New Zealand. In the Americas, P. semilanceata occurs in the northern reaches, from British Columbia to west of the Cascade Mountains in northern California.

P. semilanceata is another dung-loving mushroom and it can be found most readily in pastures and fields, especially those inhabited by cows or sheep. It appears most readily in damp areas around clumps of sedge grass or in the damper parts of fields. The best times to look for this mushroom are in the fall and early winter.

Farmer Dodds/Shutterstock.com

In the spring, it can be found in coastal Oregon and Washington, though it is rarer in these times and places than in those mentioned above. Common names for this mushroom include "Liberty Cap," and "Witches Hat."

PSILOCYBE STUNTZII

Psilocybe stuntzii, as the species described above, prefers to grow on wood chips and the decaying substratum of conifer forests. It can be found in British Columbia, Oregon, and Washington, as well as throughout the Puget Sound region. The best times to look for this mushroom are from fall to early winter. Common names include "Blue Ringers," "Stuntz's Blue Legs," and "Stuntz's Psilocybe."

Sovereign/Mushroomobserver.org

PSILOCYBE SYLVATICA

Psilocybe sylvatica has a relatively widespread distribution, appearing in Northern Europe and across the northern borders of the United States from New York to Michigan. It can also be found in Canada from Ontario to British Columbia. P. sylvatica is another wood-loving mushroom that tends to grow on wood chips and wood debris. It also tends to appear in decaying conifer substratum. P. sylvatica can be found most easily

crod321/Shroomery.org

in the fall.

PSILOCYBE WEILII

Psilocybe weilii has, to date, only been reported in a limited range in northern Georgia. Furthermore, it was only discovered after the region was affected by hurricane Opal in 1995. P. weilii is often found in red clay enriched by pine needles, especially beneath loblolly pines and sweetgum trees. It has also been found in Bermuda grass or fescue or in urban lawns and deep woods near decaying wood. In one historical instance, thousands of P. weilii were found in a clearing affected by a leaking sewage pipe. After the leak was fixed, this species was never again reported in the area.

Photo source: Trufflemagic.com

P. weilii is most likely to appear from September to November. This species tolerates temperatures from 45 to 80°F/7-27°C, though it appears most frequently when the temperatures range from 60 to 75°F/15-24°C.

COMMON PSILOCYBE CHARACTERISTICS

Though it should be evident from the images above that the different Psilocybe species vary widely in appearance, there are some characteristics which are traditionally used to identify psilocybin mushrooms. Most will have a golden color on the cap or in the center of the cap. Several have a purple ring around the upper portion of the stem, just below the cap. This is the result of a portion of the membrane remaining when the cap detaches from the stem during growth.

Psilocybes will also tend to be wide-gilled mushrooms. In many species, the gills will have a greyish color, from light to dark grey. However, the gills of some species will be lighter in color, so this cannot be used as a marker for positive identification. The same can be said for the characteristics described above. Some Psilocybes do not display a purple ring, and some have either a darker cap or a pale color without any trace of the golden hue that characterizes some species.

There is one characteristic which is common to all Psilocybe species. This is the tendency for the stem and flesh to turn bluish when broken or bruised. This may appear as a slight darkening of the flesh, or it may change color so markedly as to appear black. If you pick mushrooms in the field, you will find that your fingers become stained dark by the juices of psilocybin mushrooms.

As mentioned above, this is the result of oxidizing psilocin. The degree of bluing is a rough indication of the potency of the mushroom. However, though this is a definite indication of psilocin in the mushroom, there are hundreds of species

Joe Farah/Shutterstock.com

that are known to contain psilocybin and very likely hundreds more which we have yet to identify. It is possible that some of these mushrooms contain toxic compounds in addition to psilocin and psilocybin. Therefore, the rule of thumb is: if you are not absolutely 100% certain of the species of the mushroom, then don't mess with it.

UNDERSTANDING THE MUSHROOM

Remember that mushrooms are the fruiting body of the fungus. That means that they are just the sexual organs. The real body of the fungus is a network of underground fibers called a mycelium. The mycelium only sends up mushrooms, or "fruiting bodies," when the conditions are stressful. Stressful conditions often include lots of rain that make the soil wet and dilutes the digestive enzymes of the mycelium. They can also include excessive heat or cold, which interferes with the growth and survival of the vegetative mycelial body. Or, these conditions may be periods of dryness which separate the soil from contact with the mycelial fibers.

What does all this mean in simple terms? When you're looking for a particular strain of mushroom, you'll want to know when and where to look for it. For example, when looking for Psilocybe cubensis in the American southeast, you'll want to look in the hot summer months after a rain when the humidity is around 80% and when the temperature has been around 80°F or 25°C. You'll also want to look in cow fields, as this is a dung-loving mushroom.

That's not all. If you're gathering in the night or early morning, you can find these mushrooms in the open field. However, mushrooms can spring up, grow, and wither in the heat of the sun in a single day. So, if you're mushroom hunting in the afternoon, you'll want to explore around the tree lines where shade will protect them from drying out. Furthermore, when you find one, stop and look a bit further. If there's tall grass, move the grass aside. Remember that they grow from underground mycelial networks, so when you encounter one, there's often a ring or patch to be found.

Sounds like quite a few details, yeah? It is. When learning to gather mushrooms, you must understand their habitat, their habits, the places they like to grow, the times they like to grow, and the conditions that spur the mycelia to produce fruiting bodies. You must also understand the subtle characteristics that identify a single species and distinguish it from the many other species with similar appearances. Mushroom hunting is an art. If you can find someone to teach you this art, then take advantage of it.

One final tip, and this is perhaps the most important. If you find yourself hunting mushrooms in the wild, remember that their spores are stored in the gills. If you are visiting a field, you'll want this field to produce on later visits. So, thump the top of the 'shroom before picking it. This will send a cloud of spores down into the medium that allowed the initial growth of the mycelial network.

Equally important is to avoid damaging the mycelial network when picking the fruiting body. So, pinch the stem and break it off gently rather than pulling it out of the soil. This will make sure that the mycelium remains strong and healthy for future visits, and that it can easily produce fruiting bodies when conditions spur it to do so.

CHAPTER 8. CULTIVATION–THE BASICS

BIOLOGY AND LIFE CYCLE OF THE MUSHROOM

ABOUT THE MUSHROOM

AN OVERVIEW OF THE CULTIVATION PROCESS

STAGES OF CULTIVATION

OPTIMAL CONDITIONS

DIY VS. READY-MADE CULTIVATION KITS

RECORD KEEPING

CHAPTER 8. CULTIVATION–THE BASICS

Mushrooms are some of the most remarkable organisms on the planet, and some of the most poorly understood. Until relatively recently, they were seen as a variety of plant and included in the study of botany. However, in genetic terms, they are more similar to animals than plants. Plus, fungi are geniuses at creating biological compounds. There is so much that they have to offer, and our investigations into mycology are still in their infancy. Between edible mushrooms, medical mycology, and ethnomycology, they provide a rich ground for future study. Central to this study is the process of mushroom cultivation, and especially, for us, psilocybe cultivation.

The more you understand about mushrooms, the more effective your efforts at cultivation will be. So, before we start on how to cultivate mushrooms, we'll have a quick look at how mushrooms grow in the wild and how you mirror this in the cultivation cycle.

Biology and Life Cycle of the Mushroom

The biology and life cycle of the mushroom is a bit technical. However, it's worth soaking up all the information you can about the mushroom, how it grows and what's going on at every level of the process. When you're looking at a beautiful, healthy flush of your own mushrooms, you'll know it's been worth a bit of reading.

About the Mushroom

In taxonomy, mushrooms are classified as fungi. This is a kingdom on its own, distinct from plants (*plantae* kingdom), animals or humans (both in the *animalia* kingdom). It is further broken down into the order Agaricales and the family *Hymenogastraceae.* This is where psilocybe mushrooms fit. They used to be part of the *Strophariaceae* family, but there has been a change to separate hallucinogenic mushrooms from others.

Mushrooms have a deceptively simple lifecycle:

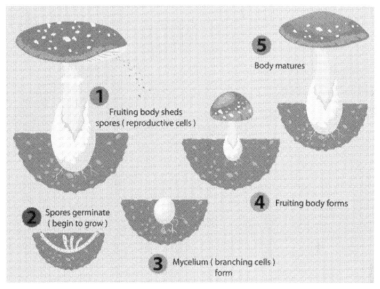

Mapichai/Shutterstock.com

The part that we see, and which we call the mushroom, is only the reproductive part of the organism. It sheds spores, which are the gametes or reproductive cells, that germinate if they fall onto the right surface. For psilocybe that means decaying matter – we call this food source the substrate.

They start growing below the surface into tubular threads called hyphae, that spread out into the substrate and divide into forks or fan-like structures. There are enzymes at the tips that break down the matter around them into separate nutrients that are absorbed into the hyphae. The system of hyphae is known collectively as mycelium and has a white, fuzzy, hair-like appearance. It will spread and cover the substrate.

The organism will stay like this until it has "eaten up" all the substrate or there is a change in temperature, moisture, light or carbon dioxide levels. This will make it send out fruiting bodies. This starts as small knotted structures called primordia, also called "pins", that start to push through to the surface of the substrate in a process known as pinning. The cells in the hyphae start to differentiate into all the parts that make up the mushroom - caps, gills, spores, stipes and so on.

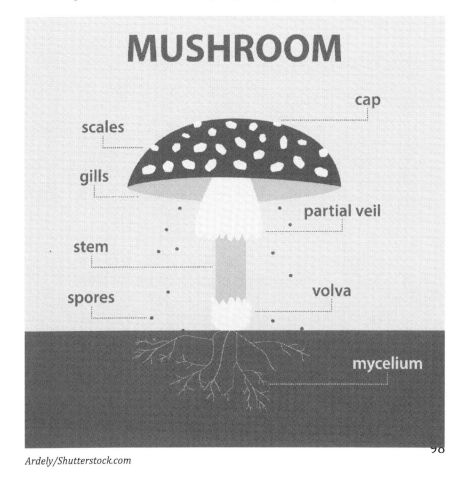

Ardely/Shutterstock.com

Pins are miniature mushrooms – they just need to absorb enough water to swell into full size. This is why mushrooms so often seem to appear overnight after rain.

So far, so good – and this may look a bit like how plants grow. So, what are the more complicated parts? Let's look more closely at the cycle:

The spores, or gametes, are housed in *gills* on the underside of the mushroom cap. These gills radiate symmetrically from the stalk or *stipe*. Inside the gills are *basidia*, little structures that look like baseball bats, and inside of these are horn-like structures called *sterigma*. There are four spores on each

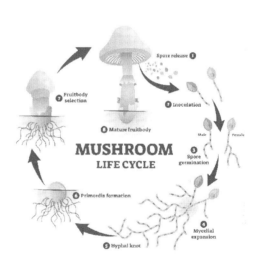

MUSHROOM LIFE CYCLE

Spore release
Inoculation
Spore germination
Mycelial expansion
Hyphal knot
Primordia formation
Mature fruitbody
Fruitbody selection
Male
Female

sperigma.

VectorMine/Shutterstock.com

However, each spore or gamete (also called haploid cells) has only half of the genetic material that is required for reproduction. When the conditions are right, each spore will start to grow mycelium as we have described. But this is only "primary" mycelium because it must find a "mate" to supply the other half of the genetic material – much like humans need both sperm and egg. Unlike humans, mushrooms have thousands of genders or mating types, and only certain types will be compatible. (We're telling you this so that when you start your own cultivation, you'll know that from a set of spores you can expect a wide variety of genetic differences.) Even when two mycelia unite, the two haploid nuclei remain distinct. It is only in the gills under the mushroom cap that the haploid nuclei fuse to form a *zygote* or a *diploid cell*. This lasts for just a short period, as the zygote immediately undergoes *meiosis*, and splits into 4 haploid nuclei which migrate into 4 new spores.

Melesandre/Shutterstock.com

As the pins grow, the stipe grows longer, the cap flattens and the membrane that connects the cap to the stalk stretches. This membrane, or *partial veil*, covers and protects the gills. When the gills expand the membrane breaks, leaving a skirt known as the *annulus* on the stem. Water condenses on the sterigma, and droplets then fall and catapult the spores out into the air. And the cycle starts again.

AN OVERVIEW OF THE CULTIVATION PROCESS

Whenever we cultivate an organism, we duplicate in a controlled setting all the conditions necessary for propagation and growth. So, having heard and understood all aspects of the mushroom life cycle in nature, it will be easier to understand the process of cultivation and the steps we take along the way.

Nature plays a numbers game, creating so many spores that one or a few are bound to work out. However, when cultivating, we are able to create conditions that favor growth. The skilled cultivator can select the best specimens from one flush to use in later inoculations, refining the species one generation at a time.

Let's look at the basic stages of cultivation. This will help you to understand how to navigate these stages and apply them to your own cultivation process.

STAGES OF CULTIVATION

All cultivation processes, whether they are indoors or outdoors, regardless of the method of cultivation used, need to follow the natural cycle of the mushroom.

There are 5 main steps in cultivation:

1. Spores

We begin with spores. You can collect your own from mushrooms growing in your area or from mushrooms you have previously

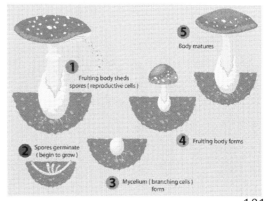

Mapichai/Shutterstock.com

cultivated. Alternatively, you may have to get some from friends or buy so-called "spore syringes."

2. Germination

You must provide suitable conditions for the spores to germinate and begin to grow a primary mycelium. The most popular method for indoor germination is to use agar as a culture medium. The resulting culture will then be used to inoculate grain or other substrates to complete the germination process.

3. Colonization and expansion

Next, you inoculate a substrate or growing medium with these cultures, allowing them to colonize to create primary spawn– i.e. the mixture of mycelium and substrate. The substrate is often sterilized grain in Mason jars. The spawn can be used immediately to move on to the fruiting stage, or it can be used to inoculate new substrate to expand the amount of mycelium you have. This is often done in spawn or grow bags.

If you are working with a strain that produces sclerotia (truffles) you will want to extend this step a bit to allow them to grow bigger, but you will skip the next fruiting step and go straight on to harvesting.

4. Fruiting

The next step in the cultivation process is to place the spawn (either primary or secondary) in conditions that promote fruiting. This includes changes in temperature, humidity, carbon dioxide and light, and generally will require a growing chamber.

5. Harvesting

Fruiting substrates will begin to produce flushes or mushroom harvests. These are then harvested, most often before the cap detaches from the stipe. A single batch will often produce three to five flushes until it must be retired, or it becomes contaminated prior to this.

This brings us full circle back to the beginning. Harvested mushrooms can be used to create spore prints or spore syringes for later inoculations. Alternately, the mycelium from the stem of a prized specimen can be used to clone mycelial cultures.

6. Processing

After the mushrooms are harvested, they are processed, either for storage or for consumption. This sixth step is not part of the natural cycle but is important for cultivators.

OPTIMAL CONDITIONS

As you may have guessed from the earlier descriptions of different mushroom species, optimal conditions will depend heavily on what species you wish to grow.

Water

In general, mushrooms prefer high concentrations of water, but not so much that they are waterlogged and subject to rot. They also need fairly high humidity levels. The best way to maintain this during indoor cultivation is through misting, using a spray bottle and through using casing layers that provide humidity. Wherever possible add a 3% solution of hydrogen peroxide to this to prevent contamination.

Light

For the germination phase, it's best to keep everything in a dark place. However, mushrooms need light to stimulate fruiting, and they will tend to grow towards the light. It's best to provide light cycles as close to natural conditions as possible. Light only stimulates their growth, rather than providing energy as it does for plants. This means you won't need much light. About 8 hours of ambient light will do the trick, and compact fluorescent bulbs are more than sufficient for this purpose.

Air

Your colonies will need to be able to breathe while still being protected from airborne contaminants. This is why filters, sterile culture techniques, and gas permeable films are so important. In fact, avoiding contaminants is the single most important factor in producing healthy colonies. The cultivation techniques offered for indoor growth and spawning are based primarily around this requirement.

Temperature

Temperature is an important factor. Wood-loving species that are cultivated outdoors are able to tolerate quite low temperatures. However, when you are working indoors, you will generally need higher temperatures. For example, if you are growing *P. cubensis*, temperatures of 75–85°F/24-30°C will promote incubation, and a slightly lower temperature below 80°F/27°C is best for fruiting. For *p. tampanensins* and *P. mexicana* where you are growing for truffles, the growing temperature should be between 70 and 75°F/21-24°C.

Growing medium

A species such as the *P. cubensis* is not very fussy about the substrata you provide. In the wild it grows on dung, but you can use anything that is high in nitrogen and carbon. This includes straw, grain, grass and even paper or cardboard if some protein is added to it. A casing layer should be added– usually this will be vermiculate or peat moss.

Other species are pickier–this is especially true for species like *P. azurescens* and *P. cyanescens* that will only grow on wood or wood chips. The truffle species *P. tampanensis* or *P. mexicana* prefer rye berries or rye grass seed, but will also grow on wild bird seed, brown rice flour and even coffee grounds mixed with coir.

DIY VS. READY-MADE CULTIVATION KITS

There are a variety of ready-made kits that you can find online. If you are a first-time cultivator or you plan to cultivate only a single batch, these kits may be the best way to go. They can also be suitable if you want to obtain a particular strain for spore syringes. Ready-made kits take most of the headache out of growing, as they have been prepared under sterile conditions and require no more than a bit of light, water, and attention. However, if you want to take your cultivation journey beyond a few flushes, then you'll want to go the extra mile. There are some challenges involved, but the benefits are more than worth the effort.

Another consideration is that all of your online activity is tracked. If you plan to do more than a little cultivation, then it's helpful to have as small an online profile as possible. In these cases, it's best to avoid buying ready-made kits or spore syringes online. While this isn't an issue for a small batch, it can lead to problems if your cultivation journey expands to sizeable proportions. Feel into it and decide what you're comfortable with.

RECORD KEEPING

This part is essential if you wish to take your cultivation journey past a few batches. In many cases, you will cultivate certain strains and fungal lines. Plus, you'll want to know what conditions work best and any situations that lead to contamination or other challenges. You will want to mark the cultures so that you can easily identify the lines. This will also help you to monitor your progress.

Note the strain, the substrate, the day of work, and the elapsed time for the batch. Over time, you'll likely create codes that indicate the originating strain and number of the current experiment, as well as the conditions that favor or interfere with fruiting.

When you make adjustments or try new innovations, write them down and track their progress. Try one new innovation at a time, so you know how it affects the success of your cultivation.

Track the speed of colonization and the speed of fruiting, taking note of the conditions of the incubating or fruiting colonies. Also note the substrate composition, inoculation techniques, and the specific Tek you use. Write down literally everything you think might have a bearing on your cultivation process. Over time, you may find that some of this information is unnecessary, and you might encounter other details that you would like to make a habit of recording.

The better notes you take, and the more organized these notes are, the more success you will have in your cultivation. This is a complex process, but you'll get the hang of it quickly. Most of all, have fun with it. Mushrooms give so much back. If you give them the diligent attention and the care they need, they will pay you back a thousand-fold.

Right, now we can start to look more closely at the steps in the cultivation process and how you can get started with growing your own mushrooms.

CHAPTER 9. CULTIVATION–UNDERSTANDING EACH STEP

Starting with spores

Germination

Colonization and expansion

Fruiting

Harvesting

Drying, curing, and storage

If you are impatient and want to move on to actually growing your own mushrooms, then you might want to go straight to **Section 3–*From Theory to Action*** outlining the different growing teks. However, where Section 3 gives you the "how," this chapter gives you the "why," and will help you understand the stages of the cultivation process in more detail.

As discussed briefly before, the following are the main steps in cultivation:

1. **Starting with spores**
2. **Germination**
3. **Colonization and expansion**
4. **Fruiting**
5. **Harvesting**
6. **Storing and consuming**

Let's take a look at some of the technical details for each step. Remember that these steps are most applicable to dung-loving species such as P. cubensis and *P. semilanceata* as well as to the "truffle" species. It is extremely difficult to get the wood-loving species to grow indoors, but many of these steps apply if you do attempt them.

STARTING WITH SPORES

The first step is to obtain a culture of the psilocybin you want to cultivate. For some methods, PF Tek in particular, the culture comes from spore syringes or spore prints.

If you are beginning your first batch, you will likely either be using a spore print from a friend or a spore syringe provided by a **friend or a company** that specializes in selling them online. If you are in an area where the mushrooms you want grow in the wild and you know how to gather them, then you may be able to take a tissue sample and clone it onto an agar or cardboard medium. Any of these sources will provide you with material to inoculate a primary substrate.

GERMINATION

You must provide suitable conditions for the spores to germinate and begin to grow a primary mycelium. You will generally do this using agar, which is a culture medium that provides good conditions for indoor germination. The typical agar blend is with malt and yeast. You could also use paper pellets or cardboard as the medium for germination. This is for getting the first germination or culture started. This culture will then be used to inoculate grain or other substrates to complete the germination and colonization process.

Part of cultivation is isolating a culture line. This is not a huge consideration for your first batch; however, it will become important as you continue on your journey. Essentially, you will want to make several samples of a mycelial culture for each generation, selecting each time for the healthiest, most robust and fastest growing individuals. You may also decide to use a piece of tissue from a healthy mushroom specimen and clone this to promote a culture line.

You will need to vary the medium in order to avoid senescence or the overuse of the line, and learn how to store and save cultures for future use.

In Chapter 13, we will give you the advanced techniques required to collect spores, germinate your own initial cultures, clone tissues, change mediums and save culture strains.

COLONIZATION AND EXPANSION

Once you have a spore syringe or a mycelium culture, the next step is to introduce it to a sterilized substrate. This is known as *inoculation*.

There are many options for substrate blends, with whole grains being ideal for *P. cubensis*. One of the simplest and most reliable recipes is a blend of cooked and sterilized whole grains and vermiculite. Vermiculite will hold water for the growing fungus, while whole grains provide an ideal food source.

The primary substrate must be carefully protected from contamination. This may be in the form of a casing material like vermiculite, peat moss or water crystals spread over the substrate and the new culture. Often, Mason jars are used to hold the grain and vermiculite. They should be covered with a material that permits gas exchange so that the fungus can get sufficient oxygen without being exposed to contaminants. This can be a cap with a filter or even a piece of cotton.

After your primary substrate has been inoculated, you will want to store it in a dark place with temperatures between 75 and 85°F/24-30°C. Colonization will occur with *P. cubensis* even at room temperature, though it will proceed more slowly.

If the ambient temperatures in your area are regularly above 85°F/30°C, you may want to wait until a cooler season. Otherwise, you'll have to build some type of refrigeration device. We haven't given any instructions for how to do this, but you can look online for some ideas. In some cases, you might have to invest in a small space air conditioner unit. Just make sure that it doesn't spread contamination, so switch it off before you open any of your containers. If the ambient temperatures in your area are lower than the ideal range, then you can build an incubator to maintain the correct temperatures.

You will see the colonies begin to form within the substrate as networks of white fibers. Allow them to grow for a few days, and then shake the jar. This will separate the grains and spread the mycelium through the substrate.

Be cautious to avoid contamination. One way is to add hydrogen peroxide to the substrate. You will want to use about 6ml of 3% hydrogen peroxide for every 2-3 cups of substrate. You can do this from the beginning if you inoculate your substrate with a mycelial culture. However, with spore inoculation, you must wait until the mycelium takes hold before adding the peroxide. Otherwise, it will destroy your spores. Shake the jar once more when it is about halfway colonized.

Full colonization will usually occur within 1-2 weeks. This combination of mycelium and substrate is known as spawn. When the mycelium completely covers the grains in the jar, you can either proceed to the fruiting stage or use this as spawn to inoculate further substrate.

If you are going to expand your spawn in this way, the first substrate is then known as the primary substrate, and the second one is the secondary substrate. The purpose of the expansion phase is to give the mycelium time and space to grow to a volume sufficient for proper fruiting.

For example, a wedge of inoculated agar medium can be introduced to a jar of grain and spread through it, creating the primary fungal spawn. In this stage, you'll need to shake the grain every few days to create space in the mixture and allow the mycelium to colonize it more effectively. The spawn can then be transferred to larger Mason jars or spawn bags filled with a grain/vermiculite mix and the incubation process is repeated.

You can do this as many times as you like until you have the desired amount of substrate. You can mix hydrogen peroxide with all spawn bags in the ratio of about 80ml per spawn bag. Make sure the substrate is as dry as possible. Follow all sterilization techniques at every step.

If you are using a wood-loving mushroom, you can mix the primary substrate with a blend of wood chips and sawdust without sterilization as they are less susceptible to contamination. You can also use a sheet of cardboard to cover the primary substrate during colonization. The cardboard becomes inoculated with mycelium and can then be used to inoculate the secondary substrate. Alternatively, you can place stems of wood-loving mushrooms between layers of cardboard and colonize them for later inoculations.

If you are working with a strain that produces sclerotia (truffles) you will want to make sure that it doesn't go on to the fruiting stage. You want to stay in this stage of growth for a longer period to allow the sclerotia to grow bigger, but you will skip the next fruiting step and go straight on to harvesting.

FRUITING

Fruiting occurs when the conditions are right, and is usually in response to a change in conditions. In cultivation, this means that you will have to slightly alter the temperature, humidity, carbon dioxide level and light. Another signal to the mycelium that it should start to fruit is if it has completely colonized its growing medium–i.e. that it has used up its nutritional source.

You will need a fruiting container for this step, and this is perhaps the step where you need to be a bit technical or you may be joining the many voices online asking why your cultures are not fruiting!

Depending on your growing method, the fruiting chamber is either filled with the secondary substrate or it is lined with perlite. The PF Tek method, for example, uses only a layer of perlite. This method is to tip colonized grain cakes/spawn directly out of the Mason jars where they have colonized directly onto the perlite layer, without breaking them apart. If they are misted regularly and provided about 8 hours of light per day, the spawn will begin to pin within a couple of weeks. Pinning is the process of creating primordia, or immature mushrooms. After this occurs, you should have your first flush within a week.

Alternatively, the colonized substrate or spawn can be broken up and spread across the bottom of a sterilized growing chamber (this is why you have used the spawn bags in the previous step, to grow the amount of spawn that you have.)

115

This substrate must be covered with a layer of casing material to protect it from contaminants and misted regularly to maintain moisture levels. Pinning and fruiting will occur within the same time frame as for the cakes, but it will be spread evenly across the growing chamber instead of collecting around cakes.

Fruiting occurs when the primordia mature into full mushrooms, often 3-6" in height. You will want to watch for the point where the veil stretches away from the stipe. The ideal time for harvesting is just before the veil breaks. Fruiting batches are termed flushes. A single growing tray will produce 3-5 flushes if you avoid contamination.

So, what can go wrong?

In some instances, the mycelium will grow over the casing material. This is known as overlay. It stops the casing layer from providing humidity and air exchange, and it prevents pinning. It can generally be prevented by returning the mycelium to incubation conditions straight after the casing layer has been added. Once the mycelium is visible on 20% to 30% of the surface, then it can be "shocked" by changing to the fruiting conditions–and it will then pin normally. If overlay has occurred, use a sterilized fork to scratch into the casing to rough it up a bit and break up the mycelium overlay, but be careful not to touch the substrate. This allows the pins to break the surface.

Temperature change is key–and whether this should go up or down to stimulate fruiting depends on the species you are growing and what they respond to in their natural settings. For *P. cubensis*, for example, the ideal temperature for germination or incubation is 75-80º F (24-27º C), but for fruiting this drops to 68-72º F (20-22º C). Managing this is easier if your normal ambient temperature is lower than these, because you can control a heating device. It's a bit trickier when your ambient temperature is higher.

Light is not needed for energy as for plants, but it is a signal to the mycelium that it has broken to the surface (as it would in its natural habitat). This is why you should provide light for only 8 to 10 hours per day to mimic the natural conditions. The light also gives an indication of the direction in which the pins should grow. So, in the PF Tek method, where the whole cake is exposed to light, the pins can come out in all directions.

The mushroom fruit is almost 90% water, so it is important to provide lots of moisture. The humidity level in the air in the fruiting chamber should be as high as 95%. However, this comes with a risk of mold. So it's important not to overwater, and rather to use a fine mist once or twice a day. Adding a 3% peroxide solution to the spray will provide some protection against contamination. The casing layer also helps to manage water. Vermiculite and glass crystals absorb water and then release it back into the substrate or the air, while perlite wicks water away and into the air.

In the wild, mycelium is exposed to very little oxygen and lots of carbon dioxide while it is underground. Once it breaks the surface the mix is changed. To mimic this, it is important to ensure that air can reach the mycelium and the growing primordia. So there must be holes in the fruiting chamber or in the lids of Mason jars or in the plastic bags often used as fruiting tents. (In mushroom growing lingo, this is often given as FAE–this simply means fresh air exchange.) To prevent contamination from the air, more sophisticated equipment has filters over the openings. For simple solutions, like a plastic bag over a bottle, the trick is to move the bag very gently up and down to allow for gas transfer without pulling in too much contamination.

Here are some tips about fruiting chambers, fruiting trays and humidity tents:

- **Fruiting trays** are simply shallow containers to hold the spawn, so the size depends on how much you are working with. Generally you will need space to have a depth of about 2–3" of substrata for small amounts of spawn and about 6" for bulk amounts. The sides should be sturdy enough to hold the substrate, dark or covered so that light does not penetrate from the side and only comes from the top, and not too deep. If the depth is too much above the substrate then holes must be drilled in the sides to allow for air exchange.

- A **fruiting chamber** may be just a large plastic bag with holes in it that the spawn or a fruiting container can fit into. It may also act as a humidity tent. Or it may be a plastic box, with holes drilled in the sides, and the holes stuffed with cotton or polyester batting material to prevent contamination while allowing for air exchange. The spawn may be placed on the base or fruiting trays are placed either on a casing mix like perlite or vermiculite or on racks in the box. The casing helps to maintain humidity in the box. If you are really serious you can build a more sophisticated unit with a humidifier and lights!

- Large plastic bags are used as **humidity tents**. They keep moisture in, but must have holes to allow for gas exchange.

HARVESTING

As mentioned above, you will harvest your mushrooms right before the veil breaks away from the stem. If you allow the veil to break, the spores will be released, and this can be a bit messy. The only exception to this is if you choose to make spore prints. If so, then allow the mushroom to spread flat before harvesting it. Remember to choose the best specimens to create spore prints, as you will want to pass those genes on to the next generation.

When harvesting your mushrooms, you should grasp the stalk and pull as much as possible out of the casing material and substrate. If you leave a portion of the stem above the casing material, it will be prone to contamination. Often this will leave a hole in the casing material. Fill this hole with casing material to protect the substrate beneath. If you disturb other small mushrooms when harvesting a mature one, remove them as well. Don't worry about the small loss of material, as the fungus will just redistribute the energy to other mushrooms.

After each flush, your colony will need more water to make up for what is lost. It will be better to mist it lightly and frequently rather than to add too much water at once.

If at any point you see contamination, don't try to save the colony. Get rid of it before it infects your other growing chambers. Mold spores can spread quickly throughout your entire growing space and contaminate it for days.

One final thing: often there will be pieces of vermiculite stuck to the base of the stem when you harvest the mushroom. It's much easier to remove these while the mushroom is fresh. You can simply scrape a knife downward against the bottom of the stipe to remove all excess vermiculite.

DRYING, CURING, AND STORAGE

There are a number of ways to store mushrooms. Fresh mushrooms can be stored in the refrigerator for about a week. It is best to put them in a paper bag or in a plastic container lined with paper towels without the lid tightly fastened. This will prevent the mushrooms from sweating and becoming soggy. If you haven't seen it before, it's not fun. Soggy mushrooms can only really be saved by brewing them into tea, and if you leave them too long, they'll mold. And that is a profound shame.

Mushrooms can be stored for months or longer if you dry them completely. You can do this in a dehydrator if you have one. Alternately, you can use a tray of rice. Place the mushrooms on top of the rice and store the tray in the refrigerator. If you have more mushrooms than a single layer, place paper towels on top of the first layer, line these with rice, and place the second layer. The rice will absorb the moisture, while the cool of the refrigerator will help to preserve the psilocin from oxygenation. Finally, you may choose to place them on a rack above a radiator. Avoid heating them overmuch, as this will break down the psilocin and reduce their potency.

Truffles (sclerotia) can be dried in a similar way. They are already much drier than mushrooms, so will dry more quickly. You can spread them out on brown paper in a warm room and speed up the process with a fan. Or you can put them in an oven at 100°F (40°C).

Dry your mushrooms until "cracker-hard" and then store them in zippered freezer bags or heat-sealed food storage bags. They can then be frozen to preserve them further. If they are handled in this manner, they can retain potency for years. The larger the sclerotia, the longer they will survive.

Fresh mushrooms can be steeped into a mushroom tea as well. Simply place the mushrooms in a pot of water and steep for up to an hour, but be careful not to boil. This will not keep as long as dried mushrooms, but it can be a convenient way to store them for up to a week, so long as the tea is kept refrigerated. Another alternative is to make an alcohol tincture. To do this, place 25-50ml of high-proof alcohol per dose in a container with your mushrooms. Allow it to soak for three days and then strain. This tincture can be stored for several months without a loss of potency.

One thing that's really cool to understand is that mushrooms are essentially immortal. Cultures can be transferred from one agar plate to the next. You can colonize paper pellets and store them in cold storage, placing them in suspended animation until you are ready to use them. Spores can also survive for very long periods if kept in airtight, cool, dry places. However, generations can tire out and become unviable after too many transfers, and even mycelia in cold storage should be warmed and grown out every couple of years, just to keep them healthy and viable.

CHAPTER 10. AVOIDING CONTAMINATION

This is perhaps the most important subject in the entire book. If you'd like to be a successful cultivator, then you will need to know about techniques to keep a sterile environment.

There are multiple contaminants in every environment. If given the chance, they will colonize and contaminate your mushrooms at every step of the way. In the best of circumstances, they will force you to discard a single growing container. In the worst, they can spread to all of your containers and force you to start from scratch. So, you'll want to take appropriate measures to eliminate contaminants.

RECOGNIZING CONTAMINATION

Throughout this book, you will read that you should be on the lookout for contamination. The question is, "What does it look like?"

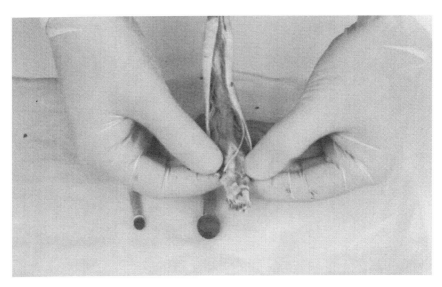

The biggest challenge is mold spores, and you will be able to see them easily due to their high pigmentation. They will look black, green, pink, or blue. Bacteria will look like sticky, wet blobs. With bacterial contamination, you'll also notice an off smell, sour or like rotten apples.

If you are trying to grow mycelium in a jar or spawn bag and the mycelium recovers slowly or doesn't recover at all after you shake it, this is a sign of potential bacterial contamination. Look for the usual sign - bubbles or wet spots.

Casing materials are generally quite resistant to contamination, and any signs of contamination may be from the substrate or from the mycelium growing through it. However, they are prone to contamination by cobweb mold or *Dactylium dendroides*. This mold starts as small white spots on the top of the casing and then becomes fluffy, and if left unattended, will cover over the entire layer, including any mushrooms that may have broken through the surface. The mushrooms will become diseased, turn brown and rot. The mold itself may become reddish brown and then yellow. It can also spread easily to other containers, so you'll want to discard any affected containers as soon as you notice it. Don't mistake the mycelium growing through the casing layer for cobweb mold, as they may look similar. Mycelium will grow through the casing and up, while the cobweb mold spreads across the casing and is very wispy.

Prevention is better than cure here. Check humidity levels and make sure there is sufficient ventilation. Sometimes a fan helps. Although it isn't necessary to sterilize casing, it might be an idea to do so if you have any concerns or if you have had any previous signs of this mold. Adding hydrogen peroxide to the water when you first prepare the casing and later during misting also helps.

Some of the "advanced techniques" are not called advanced because they are difficult to do. They are advanced because the risk of contamination is high, and you have to be super careful of how you deal with this. Working with agar to propagate your own cultures is an example of this. In fact, at the end of Chapter 13, we have given a contamination troubleshooting checklist just for agar.

If you do notice any signs of contamination in jars, plates, or growing trays, get rid of the culture. **Do not** try to rescue it. Don't open contaminated jars or bags anywhere near your workspace as they can release billions of spores. Dispose of the contents well away from your workspace and clean any re-usable equipment thoroughly before further use. It is best to sterilize them in your pressure cooker. In fact, it is sometimes a good idea to sterilize the contaminated containers before you open them to throw away the contents. Move slowly so that you don't spread spores more than is absolutely necessary. Wash your clothing and shower well before entering your workspace again.

Resist the temptation to use portions that seem to be uncontaminated. Even healthy-seeming mushrooms can absorb toxins from contaminants in their environment. At best, they will make you feel really sick. At worst...well, let's just say leave them alone.

The key is to understand sterilization and to stick rigidly to sterile working practices. Shortcuts become very long cuts!

STERILIZATION: THE BASICS

Many would-be mushroom growers have learned the hard way that maintaining sterile conditions is not an option. Getting it right gives you a chance of producing flush after flush of healthy mushrooms. Get it wrong, and you're most likely to produce only mold and bacteria.

First, you will want to thoroughly sterilize the materials and the equipment that you are using. This is to kill all mold spores and bacteria. A pressure cooker is one of the most important pieces of equipment for this purpose. Temperatures reached in its chamber are high enough to kill most bacteria and mold spores.

Use sterile water and include 3% hydrogen peroxide when you can, also when you are misting the growing or fruiting chambers. The bottle of peroxide is itself a potential contamination hazard. You should sterilize foil-wrapped glass pipettes prior to inserting them in the bottle. Also, keep the bottle sealed with plastic wrap and lid, sealed in a Ziploc bag and refrigerated between uses. Wipe it down with disinfectant before you bring it to your workspace.

Sterilize all tools in an alcohol flame between jars, plates, and containers. This helps to avoid spreading contamination from one culture to another.

Second, if you want to keep everything sterilized, you must maintain sterile working conditions. If you don't, contaminants from the air or surfaces will simply re-contaminate your materials.

TIPS AND TECHNIQUES FOR STERILE WORKING AREAS

A number of elements need to be considered here. In the first place, you need to know *what* must be kept clean and sterile, and then you need to know *how* to do it.

What must be kept super clean? You should consider everything that might house bacteria or mold spores or any contaminant that might come into contact with your substrate, spawn or growing mycelium.

Obviously, this means all working surfaces, floor areas and walls. It is better if the surfaces are easy to wash and you can quickly see signs of dirt–tiles, vinyl or laminates work well. Carpets are a no-no. Keep walls freshly painted using a latex paint. Avoid wooden tabletops. Surfaces should be washed regularly using an organic disinfectant.

You are also a potential contaminating agent. Human skin is a microbiome, colonized by a wide range of microorganisms such as bacteria, fungi, viruses and mites. Most of these are harmless to you, but you might not want to share them with your mushroom substrate and spawn. Your own personal protocols before working with your mushroom materials are therefore extremely important. The routine would be to shower, dry off with a clean towel and put on clean clothes. They should be closely fitting rather than loose or flowing. Tie back your hair. Disinfect your arms and hands–rubbing alcohol works well–and use disposable gloves that have also been disinfected or sterilized.

Not so obvious is that the main source of contamination is the air around your materials and in your working area. Keeping that clean is not quite so easy. A single cubic centimeter of air typically holds about 100,000 particles of bacterial and fungal spores. These are competitors for macro fungi like psilocybin mushrooms. This complicates working with mushroom materials as you cannot easily work with them in the open. This is why you need a flow hood to blow clean air over your workspace. Alternatively, you must work in a glovebox.

It is important to keep the air as still as possible. This means no drafts or unexpected movements of air. Doors and windows must be kept closed, fans and air conditioners generally switched off and any ducts sealed. You should also move slowly and carefully so as not to set up air disturbance and release unnecessary bacterial or fungal spores.

There should be no pets, litter boxes or food bowls, nor any plants in pots. All of these can release organic contaminants.

If you can work in a dedicated place that can be shut off from general traffic this makes your life easier. If you can't, it means that you will have to be constantly cleaning and disinfecting.

EQUIPMENT TO PREVENT CONTAMINATION

If you can afford them, there are some useful tools to keep your mushrooms and cultures free from contamination.

The first is an **air filter** to remove particles from the air.

Look for one that has the label "True HEPA." This means that it meets strict standards set by the US Department of Energy and that it will remove up to 99,97% of particles, even with a size as small as 0.3 microns. A bacterium is usually between 0.3 and 2 microns; mold spores may be between 10–30 microns and skin flakes are between 0.5 and 10 microns. It is best to keep this filter running all the time, and perhaps to set it to its highest setting for about an hour before you want to work with your mushroom material.

Instead of a full filter, or perhaps in addition to it, is a **flow hood** directly over your working surface. It blows absolutely clean air over the work area and displaces all contaminants. You can have a horizontal airflow unit , which blows air from the back toward the front of the working area, or a vertical airflow unit, blowing air from above the working area and out through the base.

This is a really useful device because with it, you can handle your materials in the open. Just remember which direction the air is flowing, and make sure to have anything potentially contaminating, including your hands, in the downstream. Also, don't have clutter on the workbench as this will obstruct the airflow.

If you don't have a flow hood, then another useful tool is a **glove box.** You can build this yourself so that you can work in an enclosed space that can be easily disinfected and can provide shelter from moving air.

When working with the glove box, use small hand motions to avoid stirring up more air than necessary.

Wipe all surfaces inside the box with alcohol to sterilize prior to use. After placing your materials in the box, spray a fine mist of 10% bleach solution to disinfect the air and outer surfaces of your working materials. Replace the lid. Allow the spray to settle for at least 5 minutes before beginning your work.

Do not lift the lids of your jars or Petri dishes further or for longer than necessary and try to keep the lid above the opening of the jar or plate. Finally, seal all jars and dishes securely before removing them from the glove box.

Throughout the book, we will be giving you information about potential contamination. However, it is best to be super alert to the risk of contamination and to take simple but systematic steps to avoid it.

Some of this equipment is quite expensive, but it is easy to build some of it yourself. Here are some ideas for building your own flow hood and glove box.

DIY FLOW HOOD AND GLOVE BOX

LAMINAR FLOW HOOD

Laminar flow means that the air is moving evenly, without turbulence. So, it's important to construct the hood correctly. You can check evenness of flow by holding a lighted candle in front of the flow at different spots in front of the fan—the angle of the flame should remain the same.

There are three parts to a flow hood: a filter, a fan and a box to house them. I'm not giving the step-by-step instructions for building the box and putting it all together as there are multiple sites online and on YouTube that do this. (I liked the very clear video on:

https://freshcapmushrooms.com/learn/keeping-it-clean-how-to-design-and-build-a-laminar-flow-hood/

However, here are some tips on what to look out for.

While building your own flow hood will be less expensive that buying one, there are two items in it that are a bit pricey, so check online or at your gardening or hardware store for what they cost before you start.

The first is the filter. It's best to use a HEPA (High-Efficiency Particulate Air) filter. The efficiency rating should be for 99.99% at 0.3 microns. Also check the static pressure–you will need about 0.1" to 0.2" For size, we would recommend at least a 12" x 24" filter, going up to 24" x 24." Smaller than that won't give you sufficient space to handle multiple jars or large spawn bags.

The second is the fan, preferably a squirrel fan. The guideline is that air should flow over the workbench at a speed of at least 100 feet per minute. To work out what size fan you need, multiply the area of the filter by 100ft/min. For a 12"x24" filter, you'll need a squirrel cage fan that blows at least 300 CFM (Cubic Feet per Minute), and no more than 500 CFM.

At current average prices, you can expect to pay between $100 and $200 each for the filter and the fan.

The box will be subject to a lot of vibration from the fan, so the usual recommendation is to use plywood–¾" to 7/8" thick. Make sure all the edges are properly airtight–use a silicon sealer if necessary.

The effectiveness of your flow hood will be further improved by creating a sterile workbench that is mostly enclosed. You can then disinfect the enclosure prior to use and set the flow hood directly in front of or above the working area.

One creative idea I have seen is to use a vacuum cleaner instead of a squirrel fan (it has to meet very stringent requirements regarding its own filtration system to ensure that there was clean air blowing through it.) This has several benefits: it's portable and has its own power supply; you can adjust the airflow; you can heat the air to sterilize the work surface; and you can reverse the airflow to suck out any dust or contamination in the working area. This same model used plexiglass instead of wood for the top and front covers of the box, and mounted a small LED light inside, so you can easily see what you are doing.

GLOVE BOX

Essentially, a glove box is a small enclosure designed to allow you to work with your cultures with minimum exposure to the contaminants that might be present in your workspace. There are many ways to build one, but the easiest is probably to use a transparent plastic container with a lid.

Materials

- Plastic container
- Knife or rotary tool to cut through plastic
- PVC pipe–2 pieces with 4" diameter and 2"- 3" long
- Tube of silicone sealant
- Elbow length rubber gloves
- Hose clamps, zip ties or strong rubber bands to attach the gloves to the PVC pipes

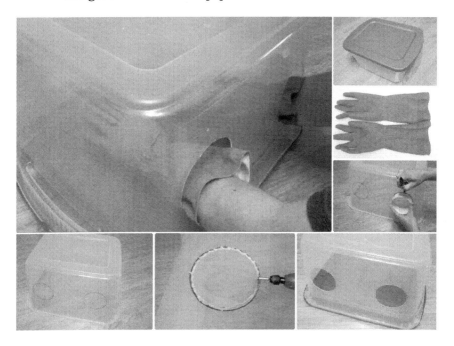

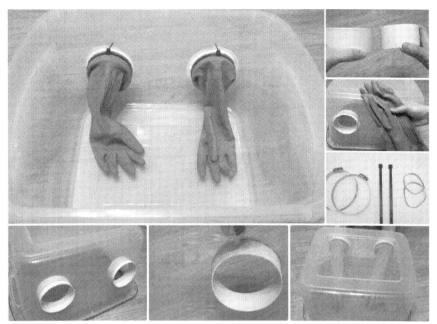

Jason Paul Smith/Instructables

Construction

1. Decide where the arm ports should be by working out where your arms will be most comfortable while working. Cut a 4" diameter hole for each arm, using a knife or rotary tool.

2. Insert the PVC pipes into the cut holes.

3. Leave about ½" of pipe sticking out of the box.

4. Apply sealant around the pipe on both the inside and the outside of the box and leave to set overnight.

5. Slide the gloves over the pipes inside the box. Check that left and right gloves are on the correct sides and that they are in a comfortable position for you.

6. Fasten the gloves onto the pipes.

What is important about a glove box is that sterile techniques must be applied before each use and after every time that the seal is broken. This means wiping down all surfaces, spraying an alcohol or disinfectant spray into the air inside and around the box, and rubbing gloves with alcohol before you commence work.

Right...now at last, we can get down to actually growing some of those wonderful mushrooms.

PART III
FROM THEORY TO ACTION

INTRODUCTION

You've now read a lot of theory about cultivating Psilocybins. If you want to take the step of actually using the theory to grow your own mushrooms, this is the section for you.

We'll first look at all the materials and equipment you might need, and we've drawn up a potential shopping list for you. Then we give you six methods for growing mushrooms, starting with the classic PF Tek and some other basic Teks and going on to magic truffles and even a wood-loving species that will usually not grow indoors.

Finally, there's some advanced technical info about propagating your own cultures–but by this time, if you've been following, you will find that they make logical sense and are not really that difficult.

This really is the best part–so let's get started!

CHAPTER 11: CULTIVATION SHOPPING LIST

CHAPTER 11. CULTIVATION SHOPPING LIST

As for any new venture, there are some set-up steps and costs associated with being a mushroom grower. Some of the cultivation techniques offered in the following chapters are designed for simplicity and require very few materials. Others are more complex, requiring a hefty shopping list. The materials described in this chapter should provide everything you need for whatever method of cultivation you choose.

The list itself is quite extensive, but don't be intimidated. If you choose to follow one of the beginner Teks offered, **look at the materials list for that Tek, and then find the necessary equipment in this list** if you need further information. If you are working with more advanced methods, plan your method out first, and then explore this chapter to learn more about the supplies that you need.

We also recommend that you just read through the chapter as we have tried to give enough information about each item to deepen you knowledge of the cultivation process itself and the reason why each item is part of it. The cultivation "Teks" we give in the next chapter will also make better sense.

Here are some pro tips: Number one is to start small when purchasing your equipment. Number two is to plan out your experiment completely before beginning. This will let you know what equipment is essential for your particular cultivation. Think about your workspace for mushroom cultivation as pretty similar to a science laboratory at a school. This will help you to understand what you will need and why, and also how best to use each item.

Overview

Here's an overview, so that if you are looking for something you'll know where to find it in the chapter.

EQUIPMENT AND CONSUMABLES

We've categorized the *equipment* according to use, as follows:

Measuring and dispensing equipment: Balance/scale; pipettes; measuring spoons, measuring cups or graduated cylinders; glass flasks or bottles; funnels; scalpel; spray bottles; marking pens.

Sterilizing equipment: Pressure cooker; alcohol lamp or mini-torch; mason jars, lids and filter discs. (In other chapters, we have given information on air filters, air hoods and glove boxes.)

Sterilizing consumables: Hydrogen peroxide, alcohol, bleach, parafilm, surgical gloves and masks, aluminum foil.

Propagation equipment: Petri dishes; spawn bags and sealers; inoculation loops; syringes; plastic containers.

Propagation consumables: Distilled water.

Miscellaneous items: Items that you probably have in your house

SUBSTRATES AND CASING:

Substrates: Agar, various grains, sawdust and woodchips, paper pellets and coir.

Supplements: Malt extract, yeast, calcium carbonate (lime), calcium sulfate (gypsum) and others.

Casing materials: Peat moss, vermiculite, water crystals, perlite.

STARTING CULTURES

This can be **spore water, spore syringes, mycelial water** or **tissue**. It can also be **colonized agar, grain or cardboard**.

Whew–long list! So buy just those things that you are going to need. Remember, this is an investment, and the payoff will be phenomenal if you follow the steps and give due diligence.

EQUIPMENT AND CONSUMABLES

MEASURING AND DISPENSING EQUIPMENT

All of the following items are fairly easy to acquire and need little explanation.

- ## *Balance/scale*

Balances or scales are used to weigh materials. You will need one that has a large enough pan to hold fairly large items, with a capacity to weigh at least 250g, but preferably up to 1 kg, and with a sensitivity of at least 0.5g. It doesn't matter whether it is mechanical or electronic.

- ## *Measuring pipette and rubber bulb*

A pipette with a rubber bulb is used to pull up and measure small amounts of liquid. You'll need one if you are going to work with agar or hydrogen peroxide, which you will see later that we recommend. It's best to buy glass pipettes so that you can sterilize and re-use them. You can buy them at homebrew stores or at specialist scientific supply stores.

- ## *Measuring spoons, cups and graduated cylinders*

Measuring spoons and cups are standard items that you will find in any kitchen supply store. Graduated cylinders are a bit more specialized and may be more accurate. They are narrow cylinders with marks to indicate the amount of liquid measured. You will probably need at least 3 of these cylinders with capacities of 10ml, 100ml and 1 liter.

You can use these items instead of glass pipettes for small amounts, but there is more risk of contamination from extra handling. As for the pipettes, it is best to use glass or Pyrex, but metal can also be used.

- ***Flasks/bottles***

You will need a flask or bottle to hold liquids such as agar during the sterilization process. As for other items, glass is best so that it can withstand the heat of the sterilizer and it can be re-used. You will also need to pour liquid out of these bottles into petri dishes, so a narrow neck is recommended. Many people use old fruit juice or alcohol bottles with screw tops. Laboratory-grade Pyrex is always better than normal glass or even baking-grade Pyrex, as they can shatter if they are either heated or cooled too rapidly.

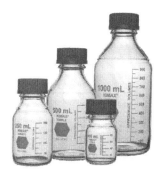

- ***Funnels***

You will need funnels to fill containers with liquids and fine powders (use a narrow-mouthed funnel for this) or with larger particles such as grains (use a wide-mouthed funnel for this).

- ***Scalpel/X-acto knife***

Scalpels are helpful for cutting tissue cultures or agar samples. They can also be used to scrape up a small section of spore print or prepare a cap to create a spore print. You can buy dissecting scalpels with thin handles and disposable blades in scientific supply stores or mushroom cultivator suppliers. X-acto knives used for precision-cutting for hobbies and crafts can also be used although they are more difficult to use in small spaces.

- *Tweezers*

You are going to need these to pick up small items and transfer from one container to another. In fact you might need two of them if you are going to try to work with spores.

- *Spray bottles*

You may need a few of these–one for spraying disinfectant onto work surfaces and into the air in your glove box, and another one for hydrogen peroxide solution that you will use to mist growing and fruiting trays.

- *Sharpies/marking pens*

Sharpies are permanent markers that can be used to write on nearly any surface. They are helpful for labeling cultures.

STERILIZING EQUIPMENT

As noted earlier, keeping everything sterile is the make-or-break of mushroom cultivation. So the following equipment is really important and we would recommend that you get the best quality you can.

- *Pressure cooker*

The pressure cooker is probably the most essential piece of equipment in your mushroom cultivation arsenal. You'll be using it regularly as an autoclave to sterilize substrates and equipment. You can buy them from grocery stores, second hand stores, scientific shops and mushroom supply stores. Both new and used models are advertised online.

The choice of make and size will depend largely on what you can afford, but there are some critical considerations to take into account:

Konjushenko Vladimir/Shutterstock.com

- Much of its use will be for sterilizing substrate in quart-sized mason jars. So buy one that's at least big enough to hold 6–10 jars.
- It should preferably have a steam release valve or "stopcock" that you can control rather than a "rocker" type that automatically releases steam if the pressure goes above a certain level. The rocker type can lead to very rapid release of pressure and steam and is likely to cause anything liquid in the pot to boil up and overflow. This can be very messy and you can lose most of your material. What you really want is for the pressure and steam to reduce naturally once the pot has been removed from the heat source. This should take about an hour and a half. It must also retain a vacuum while it is cooling, so non-sterile air cannot get in to contaminate your cultures or substrate.
- There must be an accurate dial to show internal pressure.
- Buy from a reputable source. Look for models that have a minimum number of parts that can wear out–and where you can buy spares if you need to.

Pressure cookers can be very dangerous. They can explode if the pressure gets too high. They can implode if you pour cold water over them to cool them down. It is easy to scald yourself with the steam. So safety rule number one is to read the manual and know exactly how to operate your pot.

- Make sure that it is working properly, with the lid properly sealed and locked into place. A bit of Vaseline on the rim will help to keep the lid sealed.
- Use a basket inside the pot so that whatever you put into it doesn't touch any of the surfaces. You can make a basket, using galvanized steel wire. Stand the basket on a rack or trivet to keep it out of the water. Anything standing in water is not being sterilized as the pressurized steam cannot reach it.
- There should be at least half an inch of water at the bottom of the pot. Some pots may give an amount in cups that should be used. Some of the water will evaporate in steam, and you want to be sure that there is enough left to maintain the pressure for the required period.
- Depending on the heat source you are using, check to see whether your pot can be used on a gas burner or only on a stovetop.
- Heat the pot slowly and let it cool down slowly. Doing this too fast can lead to the glass inside the pot shattering.
- Let a full head of steam develop before you close the stopcock.
- Never leave a pressure cooker unattended. Know how to operate the emergency release according to the manufacturer's manual.
- Never put a sealed container into the pot. Make sure that there is a way for air to escape through the lid.

- Finally, to ensure sterile conditions, wrap the outlet of the stopcock with an alcohol-soaked cloth prior to opening the valve. This will ensure that no spores or other contaminants enter the cooker when you vent the steam.

Most bacteria and other microorganisms are killed if you leave them in the pot for 15 minutes with the pressure at 15 PSI and the temperature at 121°C/250°F. Specifics about times required for different substrates are provided in later chapters.

- ### *Alcohol lamp or mini torch*

You will use the flame from these items for sterilizing equipment like inoculation loops and scalpels while you are working. Alcohol lamps are filled with rubbing alcohol and capped with a cotton wick and metal cap. Mini torches are generally butane-based. They are used by chefs and for soldering small items, so they are fairly easily available. They are easier to use if they have a base and can stand upright on the table top. Alcohol lamps can be found at scientific or mushroom supply shops.

- ### *Mason jars, lids and filter discs*

These are three items, but are used together. You are going to use the jars to create spawn–ie the mixture of substrate and mycelium that can then be moved to other locations to propagate mushrooms.

Graham Taylor/Shutterstock.com

You want plastic lids because you want your jar sealed, but air must be able to escape so that the jar does not explode in the pressure cooker. To modify them, cut or drill a 1-inch hole in the center. Then, fit the lid with a filter disk so air can enter, but harmful contaminants are blocked.

The filter disc is made of a synthetic fiber that can be sterilized and re-used. If they discolor from contact with substrate or mold spores, soak them in a quarter-strength bleach solution. You can buy the discs pre-cut to fit your lid, or make your own.

The pre-cut ones that are sold specifically for mushroom cultivation are very effective, with some being sold with the same specifications as HEPA air filters – i.e. 99,97% effective against microbes as small as 0.3 microns. They can be re-used multiple times.

For a cheaper option you might want to make your own using Tyvek–this is the material used for indestructible mailing envelopes. You can buy it in building supply stores. Just note that filters made from Tyvek should be cut larger than the lid and placed *over* the lid, not between the lid and the mouth of the jar. It must be tied down with elastic bands or the regular screw top outer band. Some people will place it between two lids that have had holes cut in them at the same position. The whole will meld into one piece once it has been heated in the pressure cooker. Use these discs only three or four times and then discard them.

STERILIZING CONSUMABLES

Basic consumables are disinfectants, including hydrogen peroxide, isopropyl alcohol and bleach, disposable surgical gloves and masks, parafilm to seal your petri dishes and aluminum foil to provide an extra layer of protection from contamination.

- *Hydrogen peroxide*

Discovering that hydrogen peroxide could be added to substrates and cultures to boost protection against contaminants revolutionized mushroom cultivation in the 1990's. It is just as important today.

Hydrogen peroxide is an antiseptic. It can be added to substrates and cultures to protect them from contamination, while not affecting the mushroom tissue. It is particularly useful in the hydrogen TEK method of mushroom cultivation. A low concentration of 3% is generally sufficient. Higher concentrations may damage the mycelium. Hydrogen peroxide at low concentration is non-volatile, non-toxic, non-irritating and completely biodegradable. It is also readily available and inexpensive.

One of the coolest things about using hydrogen peroxide is that it releases oxygen and water as it breaks down. This means that, in addition to reducing the potential for contamination, it will also promote growth. However, remember that a 3% concentration means that the other 97% is water. So it will be necessary to ensure that your substrate is as dry as possible to start with to prevent excess moisture.

Strength of the product may depend on its age, so it is a good idea to check sell-by dates and to keep it in properly sealed containers in the refrigerator. Pipettes or graduated cylinders that you use to dispense the hydrogen peroxide should be sterilized, at least by boiling.

On a more technical note, it's important to remember that while mycelia will grow happily in hydrogen peroxide, mushroom spores will die. So, you can use it for tissue culture (cloning) methods. However, you can't use it when you are working with spores–as in spore inoculation. Here the substrate must be sterilized through pressure and heat.

It's best, if you are using agar, to germinate spores on cardboard discs or agar plates without peroxide, and then transfer them to another substrate or agar which contains peroxide once the mycelium has formed.

The good news is that because peroxide kills spores, you can grow agar cultures and also fruit mushrooms in the same building, even though the mushrooms give off lots of spores.

- *Isopropyl alcohol*

Isopropyl alcohol or rubbing alcohol is indispensable. It is the fuel for alcohol lamps. You will also use it to disinfect containers, hands, and surfaces. We've mentioned previously how it should be used to wipe down the outsides of grow bags and the steam outlet of your pressure cooker. Using a spray bottle is the most efficient way of using it. It can be used in concentrations of either 70% or 91%. However, it must be handled with care as it is extremely flammable.

- *Bleach*

Ordinary household bleach in the form of Sodium hypochlorite (NaOCl) is readily available. It is good for cleaning and disinfecting surfaces and tools. ¼-strength is ideal for this purpose, while a 10% dilution in a spray form is best for disinfecting air and surfaces.

Some research done by the MicroChem Lab in Texas, USA, seems to indicate that adding vinegar to bleach makes it super-effective, especially for killing bacterial spores. The recommendation is to dilute one cup of bleach to a gallon of water and then add a cup of white vinegar.

- *Parafilm*

Parafilm is excellent for sealing Petri dishes. It is an elastic, paraffin-based film. Its special characteristic is that it allows for gas exchange, allowing air in while keeping out contaminants. It is sold as grafting tape in gardening shops and comes in rolls of 1" strips. Glad wrap or other polyethylene film wrap or even masking tape can be used as an alternative, but you will have to check that they are permeable to air.

- *Surgical gloves*

Surgical gloves help to keep contaminants on your hands away from your cultures. Wipe hands and forearms down with alcohol before putting them on, and then wipe the outside of the gloves with alcohol as well. Make sure all the alcohol has evaporated before you go near a flame.

- *Masks*

Sometimes when you are working with chemicals or with fine particles like vermiculite, you may need to wear a mask over your mouth and nose to protect yourself from lung irritation. You can get these at any store selling pharmaceutical products.

- *Aluminum foil*

Aluminum foil is very useful for sterilizing. Wrap utensils such as scalpels, syringes, inoculation loops and the like in foil before you place them in the pressure cooker. You can also use it to close the tops of glass containers. You can wrap petri dishes in foil to sterilize them and then leave them wrapped until needed to provide an extra level of protection against contamination.

PROPAGATION EQUIPMENT

Here is information about what you will need as you start on your journey of actually propagating mushrooms. We will describe what the roles are of petri dishes, spawn bags, impulse sealers, inoculation loops and syringes.

- *Petri dishes*

Most cultivators will use Petri dishes to germinate spores and store cultures. If used with agar, they are called agar plates. These dishes are small transparent trays, generally about 100 x 15 mm in size and made of either glass, plastic or even polystyrene, with loose-fitting covers. They are generally stacked on top of each other. The plastic and polystyrene ones usually come pre-packed in stacks and already sterilized. To use them, wipe the outer wrapping with alcohol, open one end and slide the stack out–preferably in front of clean air coming from your flow hood.

Glass or Pyrex dishes can be sterilized in your pressure cooker. They may be expensive to buy but can be used almost indefinitely. You can also use small jelly jars if you don't have petri dishes but they will take up

a lot of space.

A tip to remember if you are working with agar that has had hydrogen peroxide added to it, is that you can sterilize your petri dishes by simply washing them with a detergent, then swilling them in peroxide and placing them in the microwave until all the peroxide has evaporated. This method can't be used if peroxide has not been added to the agar.

Either use the dishes immediately or store them in a fresh plastic bag. As mentioned earlier, you can also wrap the dishes in aluminum foil, sterilize them in the pressure cooker and leave them wrapped up until you need them.

You can find Petri dishes at mushroom supply shops and scientific shops.

- *Spawn bags and impulse sealers*

Spawn bags, sometimes simply called "mushroom grow bags," are clear polypropylene bags intended to hold large amounts of spawn. They contain small square filters on one side, so they are sometimes also called "filter patch bags." They are pretty specialized and you would probably have to look for them in mushroom supply stores.

These bags have certain important characteristics:

- They have gussets–i.e. the sides of the bag are folded flat to the inside. This is a bit like the bags used to microwave popcorn. As the contents expand, so the bag is able to open up. In this case, as the spawn grows, so the bag is able to accommodate it.

- They have filter patches on the front of the bag. This allows air to pass through, but contaminants are trapped by the filter. Without air, the mushroom culture would stop growing, but if left in the open it would be taken over by contaminants.
- They are generally made of polypropylene because they must be able to withstand high temperatures, often for long periods of time. Ordinary plastic would simply melt.

The process is that you would add substrate to the bag and sterilize it. Then the substrate is inoculated with some growing mycelium and sealed with a heat sealer, also called an impulse sealer, and the resulting spawn is left to grow.

The grower can see what is happening, be on the look-out for contamination and also shake or manipulate the substrate to make it easier for the spawn to develop. The bags can be re-used a few times while they are still flexible.

Make sure that your impulse sealer is wide enough to seal the entire open side of the bag. Impulse sealers are pretty widely available, also online.

As an alternative, gallon or half-gallon Mason jars can be used to generate larger volumes of spawn. Another alternative is oven bags, though these are not ideal as they contain no filters and they can't heat-seal. If using an oven bag, you'll want to create a makeshift filter by filling the neck with cotton or Poly-fil and sealing it with a rubber band. The contents cannot be shaken without dislodging the filter, but they can be manipulated by hand.

- *Inoculation loops*

Inoculation loops, also known as smear loops, are used for picking up small amounts of mycelium or spores and transferring them to agar plates or spore syringes. They are wire loops attached to thin wooden or metal handles. You can buy them from brewmaking or scientific supply stores, or make your own from small dowels and thin, stiff wire.

- *Syringes*

Syringes are used to inoculate substrate with spores, as described in the PF Tek method. This requires fairly wide-bore needles of about 18-gauge, and a capacity of 10ml to 20ml. These can be challenging to find, as their sale is regulated in the U.S. Surgical and veterinary supply shops are one possible location. Another option is to purchase preloaded spore syringes from online suppliers and then reuse them as necessary. They can be sterilized and reused indefinitely.

- *Plastic containers*

You will need a variety of plastic boxes or containers, both for growing and for DIY equipment. In general these are medium to large size storage boxes with lids, freely available in homeware and hardware stores. Also you will need smaller shallower containers for fruiting trays.

PROPAGATION CONSUMABLES

- *Distilled water*

You are going to use a lot of water for cultivation. If you are putting the water into a pressure cooker then tap water is usually fine. But water can add contamination and chlorine is also not good for your mushrooms. So, distilled water is the answer. You might have a really good water filter in your house, and particularly one that uses reverse osmosis. Otherwise you might have to buy distilled water from a specialized water shop. Some pharmacies will have it.

MISCELLANEOUS ITEMS

There are a number of other items that you will need from time to time, but that you may have around the house. This includes cotton balls, various sizes of Ziploc and other plastic bags, plastic wrap, paper towels, cardboard, brown paper, and paper bags, mixing bowls, spoons, sieves, colanders and the like. You might even have an air temperature thermometer. If you are doing a lot of growing, you might want to keep some of these just for this purpose.

SUBSTRATES, SUPPLEMENTS AND CASING MATERIALS

A substrate is any substance on which mycelium will grow. Some are obviously better than others. In some cases, supplements are added to the substrate to provide extra nutrition for the mycelium or to improve the structure of the substrate. Casings are additional layers of material added to the top of substrates, most often to aid with water retention.

In this section, we look at agar, whole grains and wood chips or sawdust as substrates. Then we discuss malt and yeast extracts that are added as nutritional supplements and lime and gypsum that are added as structural supplements to the substrates. We will look at peat moss and vermiculite for casing, before we finally discuss...of spores.

SUBSTRATES

There are many substrates for mushroom cultivation. We are describing only our favorites here.

- *Agar*

Agar is a jelly-like substance, obtained from red algae in seaweed.

It is widely used in desserts, as a substitute for gelatin. It is also used as the base in which to culture various media in microbiology.

In mushroom cultivation, agar is used as the medium in which to culture spawn. It is generally poured into petri dishes and inoculated with mushroom spores or mycelium. Yeast or malt extract may be added. Once spawn starts to develop it can be used to inoculate grain and further grow the spawn. In the following sections, we'll explore exactly how this is done.

- ***Whole grains***

Whole grains are ideal for spawning of many mushroom types. Grains include wheat, brown and white rice, rye–and even popcorn or birdseed. Some people swear by rye, others say that white winter wheat is best. You will have to experiment to find out what works best for you.

The benefit of grains is that they are like little individual containers of water, minerals, and nutrients. Their outer husks protect them from contamination. They can easily be colonized by fungi and then easily separated from each other to inoculate other substrates like wood, straw, manure or whatever you choose. One description that I saw showed how just one liter of sterilized grain with a slice of culture from a petri dish could turn into spawn for 10 one-liter jars, then 100 jars and on to 1000 jars. This will produce thousands of pounds of mushrooms.

I would generally recommend grains with larger kernels like corn, rye, or wheat. Smaller kernels like rice and millet–and bird seed–tend to stick together once they have been cooked. Organic grains are preferable, as they are free of fungicides.

- ***Hardwood sawdust and wood chips***

Wood chips and sawdust make excellent substrates for wood-loving mushrooms like P. cyanescens and P. azurescens. Hardwood is best, as it is more resistant to contamination than softwoods. Beech, birch, oak, cottonwood and alder are the most suitable. Wood chips can be sourced from garden centers or barbecue suppliers. If you chip your own, it's best to do it in winter or early spring, as the wood will be high in sugars and low in leafy material. Just be careful that you don't use wood shavings as the shape does not pack well and mushrooms do not grow well on them. Rather use a chipper that grinds the wood quite small but not into sawdust.

Wood chips are very productive for mushroom cultivation. Mushrooms can be fruited up to three times on the same wood chips and then they can be used to transfer mushrooms to a new substrate.

Wood chips on their own may allow too much airflow and this may prevent the mushrooms from growing from one to the next. Sawdust, on the other hand, may be too fine and pack too tightly for good mushroom growth. The solution may be to combine the two–20% chips to 80% sawdust.

An easy way to find sawdust is to look for sawdust fuel pellets that are sold for home heating and for food smokers. They are made of sawdust that is pressed together under high heat, which means that they are pre-sterilized. When you add water, the pellets break down into a loose sawdust texture. Make sure to get pellets made only from hardwood sawdust.

- *Paper pellet cat litter*

Paper pellet cat litter is excellent for storing cultures. Its structure makes it ideal for maintaining rather than growing many mushroom species. You'll want to use unscented brands made of 100% recycled paper. If you want to use kitty litter as a growing medium, then most growers suggest that you add guinea pig feed to the paper to provide the nutrients needed by the mushrooms.

- *Coir*

Coir is a natural fiber from the husk of a coconut. It is used for ropes, brushes, mattresses and upholstery and is available online. It is high in sodium and potassium and needs to be buffered with calcium carbonate (lime) to adjust the pH level and make it suitable for growing mushrooms. Some of it comes pre-treated for this, so check what it is you are buying. Coir can be used as a substrate and also as a casing layer.

SUPPLEMENTS TO SUBSTRATES

- *Dried Malt Extract*

Malt comes from grains that have been allowed to sprout by soaking them in water. The germination is then stopped by drying in hot air. The result is partial conversion of starches to sugars. This product is then "mashed" in warm water to further release sugars and concentrated to produce malt extract. It is a sweet treacly substance most often used in beer brewing and for dietary supplements.

Malt extract is added to agar to add nutrients for the mycelium to absorb as it is packed with sugars, vitamin A and riboflavin. It can be sourced from brewing suppliers. Only light or tan malts are suitable. Dark malts have been caramelized, and fungi will not grow on caramelized sugars.

- *Yeast Extract*

Yeast extracts add protein, vitamins, and minerals to the agar substrate. Brewer's yeast will also work. Mix 2 to 3 grams of brewer's yeast to 10 grams of agar, and then add about 600 ml water and heat through to dissolve everything into the water. Pour into a warmed jar and sterilize in a pressure cooker.

- ***Calcium Carbonate (lime)***

Calcium carbonate ($CaCO_3$) goes by many names–lime, chalk, limestone, oyster shell and eggshell. It is an alkaline.

Mushrooms grow best when the pH of the substrate is near to neutral (pH of 7) or slightly alkaline (pH of 8). Bacteria, on the other hand, prefer an acidic environment. So you will add calcium carbonate to your substrate to adjust or maintain the pH level, but at the same time this will provide protection from contamination and add calcium as a supplement.

Be sure you are using calcium carbonate and not calcium hydroxide, also known as hydrated lime or quicklime. This can be used pasteurize straw for substrate, but should not be added to the growing medium. Also, be careful if you see that there is magnesium in your product–any amount more than 1% magnesium will interfere with fungal growth.

- ***Calcium Sulfate (gypsum)***

Calcium sulfate is also known as gypsum. It is pH neutral so does not change the pH of the substrate. Rather it is added to substrates to help them absorb water. Calcium sulfate prevents the material from becoming waterlogged and clumping together. It gives the substrate a more fluffy texture and makes it easier to separate the grains while colonization is happening.

- ***Other supplements***

Depending on the recipe you are following here may be other ingredients suggested. For example, the Fast Food of the Gods method requires **dextrose, oyster shell powder** and **glycine**. The method we describe for truffles needs **coffee**. Dextrose is a corn sugar easily available at grocery stores or at animal feed stores. Oyster shell powder is a form of calcium carbonate. Glycine is an amino acid, used by sports people to increase energy, and it can be bought in powder form at sports outlets and health stores.

CASING MATERIALS

Casing layers can use a variety of materials, including garden soil, coco coir and types of moss. The best types retain water well and resist contamination. Here we describe the ones used most commonly for psilocybe strains.

- *Peat Moss*

Peat moss can be found in any garden center, and it is used as casing for two reasons. Firstly, it retains water well so it keeps the substrate moist. This is very important as fungal fruit bodies are up to 80% moisture. Secondly, it aerates the substrate and makes it more porous. If you use peat moss, remember you will need to buffer it with calcium carbonate as it is somewhat acidic.

- *Vermiculite*

Vermiculite can also be found in garden centers. It can hold several times its own weight in water and in this wet form it is used as a casing and it may also be mixed into the substrate to provide moisture, to provide some structure and to allow for gas exchange. It is very resistant to contamination and generally does not even have to be sterilized or pasteurized. So it is sometimes used dry on top of the substrate to protect it from contaminants.

Quite often growers will use a 50:50 mix of peat and vermiculite for casing.

Be sure to wear a painter's or a surgical mask so that you don't breathe in the fine vermiculite particles, as they can cause lung irritation.

- *Water Crystals*

Water crystals, also known as hydrogels, are tiny polymer beads that swell up when they absorb water–a 10g packet of dry beads will swell to 2 cups of crystals. They can be used for casing where they will slowly give off their water as it is needed. They can be used over and over and will last for several years. They are non-toxic and completely biodegradable.

- *Perlite*

Perlite is used as a humidifier in a growing chamber. It was first used for the PK Tek method. Perlite seems similar to vermiculite, as both are used by gardeners to aerate soil. But while vermiculite is a mica, perlite is a volcanic glass. Rather than absorbing water, it traps water in its uneven surface structure. Water can then evaporate slowly, humidifying the growing area. Vermiculite has a neutral pH, while perlite is slightly alkaline. Perlite acts as a wicking system–this means that it draws water upwards to the air. This is why you must keep the water level in the growing chamber below the top of the perlite. It is only the surface exposed to the air that will allow for evaporation. Because perlite does not absorb either water or nutrients it can easily be cleaned and reused.

SPORES, MYCELIUM AND MUSHROOM TISSUE

Depending on the method you choose, you will need either some psilocybe mushroom spores, some mycelium or a piece of mushroom tissue to get started. Once you have them you can put all of your equipment and learning to good use.

The recipe might call for **spore water** (spores in water) or **spore syringes** (this is spore water in a syringe) or mycelium water (water with small pieces of mycelium in it).

This most critical part of the propagation process may also be the most difficult. While psilocybe mushrooms may grow quite prolifically in the wild, individuals cultivating them may be frowned on. In fact, in some places it is illegal for you to have them. So please check carefully what the status is where you live.

If you are lucky enough to have wild psilocybe growing nearby, then you can pick some for tissue or do a spore print to collect spores. If you are not so lucky, then you might want to find a friend who could share some of his crop with you.

The alternative is to buy spore syringes online. Be discreet when you do this and make sure that you are dealing with a reputable source that will also be discreet.

In Chapter 13 we will give you techniques to work with spores and mycelium to propagate your own starting cultures. We will also explain how to you can produce **colonized agar** and **colonized grain**, which are used in some cultivation methods.

CHAPTER 12. FIVE BASIC GROWING TEKS

CHAPTER 12. FIVE BASIC GROWING TEKS

In this chapter, we provide a few specific Teks, or mushroom cultivation techniques, to get you started. This chapter is ideal for beginners, as it is devoted to simple, low-cost methods which can be done with limited materials and experience. Plus, after you have some experience with these methods, you'll be much better prepared to move on to more complex techniques.

The focus is on indoor cultivation techniques. *P. cubensis* is the ideal species to work with for this because it is the least particular with regard to growing conditions. It will produce well under a wide range of temperature and humidity conditions and will fruit happily on several different substrates. The first is the *PF Tek*, a method made popular by Psilocybe Fanaticus in 1991. This is one of the best Teks if you are just starting out on your cultivation journey, though it is specific to *P. cubensis*.

Next, we offer a Tek known as the *Fast Food of the Gods method*, and it can be found in further detail on Erowid. Also on this site is a detailed description of a technique called the *Psilly Simon's Tek* which can be found in *Psilly Simon's Mushroom Growing Guide*.

The forth Tek is for the cultivation of mushrooms that produce both sclerotia (psilocybin truffles) and mushroom fruit bodies. And finally, we have a Tek that is for growing a wood-loving species indoor thanks to Trufflemagic. This is notoriously difficult to get right, but the steps are quite straightforward and by the time you get to try it, you will have learned a lot of the techniques from the earlier Teks.

Each of these Teks is relatively simple, and they are provided so that you can get going before you have gathered extensive materials and equipment.

We also provide an estimate of the cost and relative complexity of the first few Teks.

INDOORS VS OUTDOORS

This book focuses on indoor growing. Indoor growing is more controlled, and the best species for beginners who want to grow indoors is *P. cubensis*. It's hardy, sufficiently potent, and can grow on a variety of different mediums. *P. cubensis* is also really flexible about growing conditions. Hands-down, it's the best strain for novice indoor growers.

However, some of you may want to try to cultivate some of the species that usually require outdoor cultivation. Your choices are limited by the climate of the place where you live. Outdoor growing is best with wood-loving mushrooms, but they will only grow if your region drops below 45°F/7°C for a few months each year. So, if you live in a warmer place, this won't work for you.

If you do live in places where wood-loving Psilocybes grow naturally, you may wish to go for an extremely simple growing method. If you can find a healthy colony of wood-loving Psilocybes, you can simply transfer a portion of inoculated mycelium to a fresh substrate and then tend the bed. This is relatively easy. Just make sure it doesn't dry out in the summer months.

Make sure that you transfer enough mycelium to colonize the substrate, and try to do it in autumn or early winter. If you cannot transfer the bed by about January, wait until the heat of the summer has passed, and transfer it then. You may not get a flush that year, but if you tend it well, you'll get a flush every couple of weeks when the temperature drops again. The mycelium will go dormant in the extreme cold, but it will come back next year if it has sufficient substrate material. Plus, the wood-loving Psilocybes are relatively potent, so if you establish a strong bed and dry what you don't need, you'll be supplied with mushrooms all year.

However, even if you live in a nice cool place, you'll probably want to make your first batch indoors. The methods for creating primary spawn are exactly the same for both indoor and outdoor growing, and you'll want to master them before you set out on more complicated methods. At the end of this chapter, I've provided a Tek for the wood-loving *P. cyanescens* to be grown indoors. No guarantees, because growing wood-loving species indoors is not easy, but you might want to give it a try.

PF TEK

For most growers, the PF Tek method of cultivation[4] is the first that they come into contact with, and it's excellent for familiarizing yourself with the stages of the cultivation process. It is designed to simplify the process as much as possible and reduce the risk of contamination to almost nothing. At the same time, Psilocybe Fanaticus devised this method prior to Rush Wayne's discovery of the benefits of hydrogen peroxide for mushroom cultivation. Therefore, I include some details which deviate from the traditional Tek and explore how to incorporate peroxide in the process.

One of the innovations of the PF Tek method is to add vermiculite to the grain substrate. This gave the mycelium more space to grow and was a better match to its natural growing conditions. It also eliminates the use of the secondary substrate altogether. Instead, it uses colonized cakes of grain spawn placed whole in a growing container lined with hydrated perlite. When the perlite is fully colonized, it is very resistant to contamination. This method has no risk of overlay, as the cakes are not covered with casing material in the growing chamber. It produces a nice flush in about six weeks and then delivers subsequent flushes about every two weeks until the substrate is exhausted.

The PF Tek method is designed for use with spore syringes, but it can be adapted to use agar cultures if desired. If you choose to go this route, you'll need to be more careful with sterile culture techniques. At the same time, if you use agar you can include hydrogen peroxide in the substrate from the beginning, which somewhat balances things out. Finally, this

---

[4] Robert McPherson (1991): *Psylocybe Fanaticus Technique/*http://www.fanaticus.com/ (accessed January 23, 2019)

method is excellent for producing a pure fruiting strain, which can then be cultured on agar plates for use with other methods.

The downsides of the PF Tek method include relatively low yields and the need for the use of spore syringes. The low yield is a result of the primary substrate. The traditional PF Tek makes use of a mixture of vermiculite and brown rice flour. This has less nutritional value than an equal volume of other grains like wheat berries, so the colony will not fruit as abundantly as it might with a more nutrient-rich substrate. The use of spore syringes is a challenge if you purchase them online, as this always leaves a paper trail. Finally, this Tek is unsuitable for any species **but** *P. cubensis*. It's a great starting point, but you'll want to evolve beyond it fairly early in your journey.

Without further ado, let's get into it:

OVERVIEW OF THE METHOD

With PF Tek, you begin by mixing 2/3 cup of vermiculite with ¼ cup of brown rice flour for each ½-pint Mason jar. About ¼ cup of water should be included per jar. This is covered with a thin layer of dry vermiculite, followed by a few layers of aluminum foil. The jars are then sterilized in a pressure cooker or boiling water bath.

Note: *This Tek is the only method which make use of the boiling water bath. In fact, this is one of the advantages of the PF Tek method. You can proceed even without a pressure cooker. However, you'll improve your results if you use a pressure cooker, should you have one at hand.*

After the jars are sterilized and allowed to cool, the aluminum foil is removed and they are inoculated with spore water at several points around the top of the jar. The layer of foil is then replaced, and the jars are allowed to incubate in a dark, draft-free place with a suitable temperature. The spores then germinate to produce a mycelium, which colonizes the jar. Since the mass spore method is used, multiple strains result from inoculation and compete to colonize the substrate. This early competition usually results in a hardy fruiting strain. Occasionally, two or more strains will colonize portions of the substrate resulting in a multi-strain colony.

After colonization, the rice cakes are knocked from the Mason jars and placed in a growing tray lined with moistened perlite. You'll want to use either a clear terrarium or a relatively shallow growing tray that can be placed into a clear plastic bag. This is because the cakes should receive light along their length as well as the top. The cake will fruit from all areas of exposed mycelium, top and sides.

Make sure that the growing chamber receives at least a few hours of light per day (8 is best) and that it is kept well-ventilated and humid. Within a few weeks, primordia will form and then shoot up into mushrooms ready for harvest. After harvesting, you'll want to mist more regularly to replace water lost from the harvested mushrooms. In another couple of weeks, you should have another flush. This should continue for another few flushes, so long as you can avoid contamination.

DETAILED INSTRUCTIONS

Materials

- ½-pint Mason canning jars with lids (either tapered or with the mouth as wide as the body)

- Brown rice flour (without preservatives. This can be easily found at health food stores. For higher yields, you can grind your own flour from organic wheat berries.)
- Vermiculite (coarse-grained works best.)
- Large boiling pot or pressure cooker
- Measuring cup
- Aluminum foil
- Hammer and small nail
- Measuring cups and mixing bowl
- Spore syringe (See Chapter 13 for information on creating or obtaining spore syringes.)
- An aquarium or large plastic box with a lid for a growing chamber/terrarium
- Perlite–enough to line the bottom of the box to a depth of 1.5"
- Sieve
- Paper towels
- 3% hydrogen peroxide solution and a spray bottle

Phase I: Sterilization

1. Decide how many jars you will use, based on the size of the growing chamber that you have. Make sure that you have enough space to hold the colonized cakes from all of the jars. At the same time, it's worth it to prepare a few extra jars in the event of contamination.

2. Prepare the lids of the jars by punching four small holes in each with hammer and nail. The holes should be placed at north, east, south, and west about 1cm inward from the edge of the lid. Punch the holes down

from the top so that sharp edges are not in contact with aluminum foil in later steps.

Photo Souce: Fanaticus.com

3. Measure 2/3 cup of vermiculite, ¼ cup of brown rice flour and ¼ cup of water per jar. Mix well in a clean mixing bowl, until the substrate is uniformly moist.

4. Fill the jars up to ½" from the top. Do not pack down. The jars colonize more quickly and are less prone to contamination when the substrate is loose. If you find that you run out of substrate before filling all of the jars, either mix more substrate or discard the remainder. It is important for inoculation purposes that all jars are filled to ½" from the top.

5. Clean all substrate material from the top ½" of the jar. Use a finger first and follow with a clean, moistened paper towel. Dry with another clean paper towel. This helps to prevent contamination.

6. Fill the remainder of the jar with pure vermiculite to act as a casing layer. Make sure the vermiculite is level with the top of the jar. The casing layer protects the substrate from contaminants while allowing gas exchange.

Photo Souce: Fanaticus.com

Note: *In the photo, the black tape is the depth for the dry vermiculite. The masking tape shows where the pf substrate goes. The top layer of dry vermiculite must be between 1/2" to 2/3" deep to provide protection from contaminants entering from above.*[5]

7. Place the lids onto the jars. If you use two-piece metal lids with rubber seals, you can orient the rubber seal upward against the lid so that the seal is not too tight. However, with the holes, this is not absolutely

---

[5] Fanaticus.com (accessed January 23, 2019)

necessary. Cover the tops of the jars with a sheet of aluminum foil and crumple it around the top of the jar. This will prevent water from entering the jar through the holes during heating. If you have punched the holes upward from the bottom of the lid, be careful to prevent the sharp edges from ripping through the foil. If necessary, a second or third sheet of foil can be added.

8. Sterilize the jars either in a pressure cooker for 30 minutes at 15 psi or in a boiling water bath. In either case, make sure that the jars do not rest directly on the bottom. If you use a boiling water bath, place a washcloth on the bottom of the pan and fill it halfway with water. Place the jars on the washcloth so that they do not rest directly on the bottom of the pot. Cover the pot with a lid and bring the water to a boil for one hour. Make sure that the jars do not float in the water.

9. Remove from heat and allow the jars to cool to room temperature in the covered pot.

Phase II: Inoculation

1. Remove the foil from a jar and set it (face down) to the side. Heat the needle of the syringe until red hot and then allow it to cool. Shake the syringe to distribute the spores throughout the water. Insert through a hole and into the substrate mixture and against the edge of the glass. Inject a small amount (about ¼ ml) of spore solution.

PF TEK

177

Photo Souce: Fanaticus.com

2. Repeat this process through the three remaining holes. Replace the foil. Each jar should receive about 1ml (1cc) of spore solution. Repeat with all jars, sterilizing and shaking the needle between each. If you use a bit less than 1cc for each, then a single 10ml spore syringe can inoculate a dozen jars.

Phase III: Germination and colonization

1. Place inoculated jars in a dark, draft-free place with a temperature that ranges from 75-85° F/24-30°C.

2. Wait for complete colonization, inspecting the jars from time to time to make sure there are no signs of contamination. Discard any contaminated substrate well away from the working area.

3. It may take as long as a month for the jar to become colonized. You will see the white mycelium grow until it surrounds all substrate particles and the entire jar shows white. If you'd like to speed the process up, you can shake the substrate after the mycelium begins to show and again after the jar is halfway colonized.

Phase IV: Fruiting

1. Prepare a fruiting chamber. Drill holes in the sides of the plastic box to allow for air exchange. Fill a strainer or sieve with perlite and soak it in a water for 5–10 minutes. Drain, and then line the bottom of the box with the perlite. Remember that the job of perlite is to allow the water to evaporate slowly and humidify the growing area. So, keep the lid on the box once you've loaded the spawn.

2. After a jar has been completely colonized, unscrew the lid and remove the vermiculite, making sure not to

gouge into the substrate. This is only to keep the growing chamber tidy, so you can leave the bits that are stuck to the colonized rice cake.

Photo Souce: Fanaticus.com

3. Turn the jar upside down and knock it onto a tabletop to slide out the cake. Be as gentle as possible. Usually, the cake shrinks slightly during colonization, so not too much force should be necessary. If you can knock it directly into your perlite-lined terrarium, this is best. If not, make sure your hands are clean and the tabletop is sterilized. Use gloves if possible, and handle the cake as little and as gently as possible. Some people suggest that you place a small piece of aluminum onto the perlite underneath each cake.

4. Make sure that all sides of the cakes are exposed to light and receive sufficient ventilation. Even a few minutes will be sufficient to trigger fruiting and show the mushrooms where to grow, but it's best to have at least a couple of hours. You'll also want to moisten the cakes lightly with a 0.3% solution of hydrogen peroxide a couple of times a day. Watch the perlite to make sure that it doesn't dry out, and make sure that you don't overwater.

Primordia will begin to form from a few days to a week after the cake has been placed in the growing chamber. They will appear first as small projections about the size of a pin. The heads will then turn dark brown, and they will grow to the size of marbles. Next, they will unfurl and become more slender as they develop into young fruiting bodies. If it takes longer than a week and a half, then the conditions are a bit off. Check temperature, humidity, and light to make sure they are on point.

Phase V: Harvesting

If the conditions are right, the cakes will steadily produce mushrooms. If they come in a flush, you can expect about 4-6 average-sized mushrooms per cake. They may also produce mushrooms one at a time, usually one per week. You can expect the same yield overall, whether they are produced individually or in flushes.

The mushrooms are ready to harvest right before the veil breaks away from the stem. Avoid the temptation to allow them to grow too large. This won't add much psilocybin to it, and

Photo Souce: Fanaticus.com

it uses a lot more of the substrate nutrient. When harvesting, you will want to remove the stem as close as possible to the cake without touching or gouging it. Keep an eye out for

182

contamination. If you notice any signs, remove the cake (gently!) and discard away from the working area. Also, discard the cake when the mushroom production significantly slows or comes to a stop.

TROUBLESHOOTING

Mushrooms will fruit from 75-85° F/24-30°C. Mushrooms will grow faster at higher temperatures, but make sure that the temperature does not rise above 85°F/30°C or the cake will revert to a vegetative state. Below about 75°F/24°C, fruiting will not be triggered.

If primordia do not form, but the cakes develop lots of fluffy mycelium on the surface, then the humidity is too high. Lower humidity and/or increase ventilation. If the primordia form but have fuzzy mycelium growing on top, then humidity is too low. Mist more frequently and make sure the perlite is sufficiently moistened.

COSTS AND CONSIDERATIONS

The very first time you cultivate with PF Tek, you may have to buy the jars, construct a growing chamber, get lights, etc. If you have to supply all necessary materials, then you're looking at maybe $100 of initial investment. For subsequent efforts, you can produce cakes for as little as a few dollars–no more than the cost of the substrate (and maybe the spores). You can keep costs down by saving the syringe and creating your own spore water from spore prints, though this will require careful sterile techniques.

FAST FOOD OF THE GODS METHOD

OVERVIEW OF THE METHOD

All right, aspiring cultivators! Welcome to the absolute simplest Tek you can find. You may ask why I didn't place it first. Well, the thing is that it has some warnings associated with it, so **you have to be extremely careful**. Another downside is that it takes quite a large amount of inoculum to grow; 5-15ml, as opposed to the 1-2ml required for a PF Tek jar. Plus, you're not going to learn very much from growing this way. But, if you just want to create a single batch, this *might* be the way to go.

This Tek[6] uses a single container and a microwave. It has the least steps of any cultivation method, and you can inoculate the substrate with either spore solution or mycelium water. You can make this for yourself by simply adding extra distilled water to a colonized grain jar and then drawing it out with a syringe. (See Chapter 13 for the exact instructions.) It's a bit of a quick and dirty method, but it suits this particular Tek.

Adding a bit of peroxide into the mycelium water will help to destroy any contaminants that may have got into the water. Remember **not** to add peroxide if you are using spore water.

---

[6] Fast Food of the Gods Method/https://www.erowid.org/plants/mushrooms/mushrooms_cultivation8.shtml (accessed January 23, 2019)

DETAILED INSTRUCTIONS

Here are all the phases of the process, the material and equipment you will need and the steps to follow.

Phase1: Sterilization

Materials and equipment for sterilization

- Microwave
- Container (with cover) that will hold all the ingredients and fits into your microwave (Rubbermaid or Tupperware products will work well)
- Spatula
- Painter's mask
- 1 cup distilled water
- 2 cups vermiculite
- ¼ cup organic brown rice flour
- ½ tsp oyster shell powder
- ½ tsp dextrose
- ½ tsp trace minerals (Gypsum will work, as it is pH neutral and this recipe includes no acidic ingredients.)
- 500mg glycine

Note: Almost all of these materials are available at health food stores and grocery stores. Dextrose can also be found in brewery shops or obtained from diabetic suppliers.

Steps for sterilization

1. Place vermiculite in the microwaveable container.

2. Take out about 20% of the vermiculite and keep it aside.

2. Add water slowly and mix with a clean spatula. When the vermiculite seems to have reached full capacity and a little water is left in the bowl, add the balance of vermiculite that you kept aside. This will usually absorb that bit of extra water and get all the vermiculite to "field capacity" where it is neither too wet nor too dry.

3. Mix together all remaining dry ingredients and add to the container. Continue mixing until all vermiculite particles are coated with dry ingredients.

4. Spread mix evenly over the bottom of the container.

5. Cover the mix with ½" to 1" dry vermiculite. (Wear a painter's mask when handling dry vermiculite).

6. Sprinkle a bit more water over the surface of the mixture, and then microwave on high for 8 minutes with the top slightly off of the container.

*Note!!!!!!!: **Fire Hazard!** Not all microwaves are the same. Some people have completely ruined their microwaves or even started fires with this method. You **must** be careful. Stop the heating process if you see **dry sparks**. You may also wish to use **finer vermiculite**, as some have found that coarse vermiculite is a greater fire hazard. Add a bit more water to the surface. Watch it!*

Phase 2: Inoculation

Materials and equipment for inoculation

- Mycelium water or spore water
- Syringe
- Butane burner or lighter

Steps for inoculation

1. Allow the container to cool to room temperature in the microwave.

2. Remove it and inoculate with 5-15ml of spore water or mycelium water. Give several squirts of the solution around the edges and along the middle.

Notes: Make sure that you have sterilized the needle of the syringe in an alcohol burner or lighter flame and allowed it to cool before inoculation. Don't forget to shake the needle before injecting the solution. This will help to ensure an even distribution of spores or mycelial tissue within the solution.

Phase 3: Germination and Fruiting

Materials and equipment for germination and fruiting

- Aluminum foil
- Hydrogen peroxide solution (10% hydrogen peroxide, 90% water)
- Distilled water
- Spray bottle
- Perforated plastic bag, large enough to hold the container (optional)

Steps for germination and fruiting

1. Wrap the outside of the container with aluminum foil, leaving the top open.

2. Place the container where it receives at least a bit of ambient light, and let it do its thing. (Optional: you can

place the container inside a perforated clear plastic bag to act as a grow tent. This will reduce the potential for contamination.)

3. Mist lightly with sterilized water when the casing layer appears dry. After fruiting begins, you can switch to 0.3% hydrogen peroxide.

4. You may wish to check the container regularly for dryness in the casing layer or signs of contamination. However, for the most part, it should take care of itself.

Phase 4: Harvesting

Steps for harvesting

1. Harvest mushrooms just before the veil breaks. Grasp the mushroom at its base, twist slightly and pull. Some vermiculite may come with it.

2. Fill holes in the casing layer with fresh, dry vermiculite.

3. Mist regularly to replace the water in the casing.

The authors of this particular Tek claim that these containers can flush for months. They also advocate placing sterilized cow dung and water in the container when the substrate looks like it is becoming exhausted.

This is a Tek I haven't tried myself, but I include it for those who want to spend as little time, money and attention on the cultivation process as possible, while still having the potential to harvest mushrooms. Give it a go, and get back with me. I'd love to hear about your results. And **PLEASE** be careful with your microwave!

TROUBLESHOOTING

The whole point of this particular Tek is that it sidesteps the complicated stuff. Initial costs are minimal. Almost nothing, if you have an appropriate container in your kitchen. You must have either mycelial water or spore syringes. And, you have to have vermiculite. Finally, it's not going to work well if your ambient temperatures are above or below optimal (75-85°F/24-30°C).

Basically, if your ambient temperatures are within this range and you have plenty of mushroom stems to make mycelial water, there are few downsides to this method. It's great if you are working with a limited budget and with less than sterile conditions. Mycelial water also allows you to introduce peroxide to the substrate from the beginning, which will vastly increase the success of this particular approach. If you do use mycelial water, any misting you do should be with 0.3% hydrogen peroxide solution (1 part 3% hydrogen peroxide with 9 parts distilled water).

COSTS AND CONSIDERATIONS

Costs are minimal. If you have the mycelium, vermiculite, and brown rice flour, this Tek will cost you nothing. If you're not careful with your microwave, it can cost you a new one and potentially costly repairs after a kitchen fire. **Please be careful!**

Under the best of conditions, if you have the spore syringe or a colonized cake to make the mycelium water, this Tek may cost a couple of dollars' worth of substrate. Several buckets created in this manner can give you high returns from an extremely low investment. They can also breed a ridiculous number of contaminants and produce absolutely nothing but trouble. It may be worth a try but know the risks beforehand.

PSILLY SIMON'S METHOD

Here's another method[7] designed to simplify sterile culture techniques.

OVERVIEW OF THE METHOD

This is an innovative technique, and one a bit different from those described above. It uses spore prints rather than spore water, and you'll get to use equipment like a pressure cooker, inoculation hoops and a glovebox, even if it is a makeshift one. The casing layer is added only after the mycelium has started to grow. It also has a very simple fruiting technique using Ziploc bags to prevent contamination from the air, but also to allow for easy misting and air movement to each jar.

Psilly Simon's Method can be considered a medium-complexity, medium-cost Tek. It requires no more than $100 if you have to buy a pressure cooker and jars, and significantly less for the second round (again, little more than the price of substrates). It is also designed for a higher yield, though you'll need the space to incubate and fruit.

Where we've thought it will be helpful and without changing the author's method, we've added a few extra ideas and tips learned from other Teks.

As for the other methods, we give you a list of all materials you will need at the start of each section. If you want to go shopping for everything at once be sure to read right through to the end of the Tek.

---

[7] Psilly Simon: Psilly Simon's Mushrooms Groiwng Guide
II/https://erowid.org/plants/mushrooms/mushrooms_cultivation19.shtml (accessed January 23, 2019)

Detailed instructions

Phase 1: Sterilization

Materials for sterilization

- 1200ml organic whole grain rye (easily found at a health food store)
- 1 bag of casing mix (perlite, peat moss, or vermiculite)
- 1 gallon distilled water

Equipment for sterilization

- Pressure cooker (find one that can manage 15 psi and hold at least 4 quart-sized jars)
- 12 quart-sized canning jars (wide-mouthed with 2-part metal lids)
- Aluminum foil (optional)
- Antibacterial soap
- Lysol (or rubbing alcohol)

Notes for sterilization

Make sure you are clean and your workspace is sterilized. (With Lysol in this Tek, though alcohol or bleach should do the trick just fine). Wash all equipment with antibacterial soap before you use them. Follow the manufacturer's specifications for operating the pressure cooker. You don't need distilled water in the pressure cooker.

Steps for sterilization

1. Place 100ml rye grains and 175ml distilled water in three jars. Place lids upside down over the mouth of the jars.

3. Moisten casing mix to field capacity, and loosely fill a fourth jar with it. Screw the lids on **loosely** (or leave lids aside and crimp aluminum foil over the top). If the jars cannot release air, then they will explode in the pressure cooker.

4. Place jars in the pressure cooker. Let the steam build before closing the pressure valve. Sterilize at 15 psi for 1 hour. Remove from heat after 1 hour and allow cooling to **room temperature** before removing the jars.

5. Tighten the lid of the substrate mix jar and set aside. Shake the rye jars to loosen the grains.

6. Repeat for as many jars as you would like to process, ensuring that you have one casing mix jar for every three of organic whole grain rye.

Phase 2: Inoculation

Materials and equipment for inoculation

- Spore print(s) in Ziploc bags
- Alcohol lamp, lighter, or mini torch for sterilization
- X-acto knife (to be used as a scraper for spore prints. You can use an inoculation loop if you have one)
- Tweezers

Notes on inoculation

According to the author of this method, the trick to avoiding contamination is to keep everything closed as much as possible. Open the lid of the jar just a crack and have it open for a maximum of 2 seconds to deposit the spores, never move the spore print out of its bag, don't lean over the jars when the lids are open.

As before, make sure that you and your work area are clean and surfaces are disinfected. If you have touched a jar (for example to loosen a lid) wash your hands again.

Steps for inoculation

1. Sterilize the scraper and the tips of the tweezers in the flame until they are red hot. Allow them to cool.

2. Use the tweezers to open the spore print bag and hold it open and use the scraper to carefully collect some spores from the print. If you can see anything, that means you've picked up thousands of spores–they are really tiny.

3. Open a jar just a crack (avoid standing over it when you do this) and immediately transfer the spores to the inside of the jar. Close the lid of the jar and screw on tightly. Repeat with all jars. Close the bag containing the spore print as soon as possible.

4. Shake all jars to evenly distribute the spores.

5. Loosen the lids *slightly* (**Important!** If lids are too tight it will prevent gas exchange and the mycelia will die).

Phase 3: Germination

Materials and equipment for germination

- Styrofoam cooler (large enough to contain the jars you plan to inoculate)

- Transparent plastic panel cut to fit over the cooler (easily found at a hardware store, and easily cut with scissors).
- Roll of plastic wrap (Saran wrap)
- Spoon
- Sterilized casing material
- Ziploc bags (sandwich size)
- Aluminum foil

Notes for germination

No surprises here. The trick is to keep everything clean and sterilized and COVERED.

Steps for germination

1. Place all jars in the Styrofoam cooler to incubate. This will take from 1-2 weeks, so long as you are in a place with ambient temperatures of around 75 to 85°F (23–29°C). The author of this method was not too concerned about exact air temperatures, as long as you avoid placing the cooler near a heater or air conditioner.

2. You should soon start to see the fuzzy white mycelium growth. Shake the jars at about 5% and 50% colonization. If you notice signs of contamination (anything that is not white), discard the contents well away from the workspace. Do not try to rescue it. It's not worth it. Plus, you should have more jars than you need with this preparation.

3. Once the jars have been colonized–you'll know this when the jar is all white - take them out of the cooler. It is time to place 1.5" to 2" of sterile casing material on top of the grain. You have a couple of options here:

Option A: **Make a temporary glovebox**.

Turn the cooler sideways. Line the inside of the cooler with plastic wrap and spray it with Lysol or 10% bleach solution. Wipe the jars to disinfect them and place them back in the cooler. Cover the opening with plastic wrap and spray it too. Allow it to settle for about 5 minutes. Cut two holes in it to fit your hands through. This forms a makeshift glovebox.

Wash hands and spoon with antibacterial soap. Using a clean spoon, load sterilized casing material on top of the grain to a depth of about 1.5" to 2." Wash or sterilize the spoon between jars.

Option B: **Tip the casing into the rye jars**

Remove the jars from the cooler and screw the lids tight. Wash the outsides of the lids and jars and sterilize with Lysol. Unscrew and remove the screw portion of the lids of both rye jar and casing mix jar, leaving the dome portion in place. Place the casing mix jar upside down on top of the rye jar, making sure that the mouths of the two jars line up. Slide the dome parts of both jars partially to one side, so that a bit of casing mix falls into the rye jar. Be careful not to let too much fall into the rye jar. Slide both dome parts closed and screw the rye jar *lightly* closed. Repeat this process for all jars. Wipe away any casing that has fallen onto the sides of the jars.

4. Wrap aluminum foil around the jars covering everything except for the mouth. Remove the lid and place a Ziploc bag over the mouth. Do not close or band the bags. They should be loose around the top so that gases can enter and leave freely, but nothing can settle directly on the mouth of the jar. Later, you will hydrate the jars by poking the nozzle of the spray bottle upward past the outer edge of the bag. You can also facilitate gas exchange and provide ventilation by slowly moving the bag up and down.

5. Place the jars in the upright cooler and cover it with the plastic panel. Remember to wash and sterilize it first. Make sure to space the jars as far apart as possible to reduce the risk of spreading contamination, should it occur.

Phase 4: Fruiting and harvesting

Material and equipment for fruiting and harvesting

- Spray bottle with a mist setting
- Distilled water
- Hydrogen peroxide
- Tweezers

Notes for fruiting and harvesting

As for the germination phase, the trick is to keep everything covered as much as possible. Even when misting the contents of the jars, the Ziploc bags should be left in place and moved just sufficiently to fit the nozzle of the spray in.

This Tek provides the first flush at about 2-3 weeks after you have added the casing mixture. The jars will continue to fruit for 1.5 to 2 months.

Steps for fruiting and harvesting

1. Spray distilled water (or 0.3% hydrogen peroxide solution) into each jar daily. Be careful not to overwater, and only lift the bag far enough as is necessary to allow the water to enter. Also, aerate bags slowly to reduce the amount of contaminant pulled in by the movement of air.

2. Give the jars from 8-13 hours of ambient light. Electric light is fine. Avoid direct sunlight, as this can cause overheating.

3. If small bits of mycelium grow through the casing spray them just a small bit to knock them back (be careful not to overwater the casing soil, as this will cause it to pack down).

4. Some mycelium may grow on the jar itself, even above the casing. Don't disturb them as they seem to produce well.

3. Examine the jars daily and watch out for mold. Discard any jars that show signs of contamination. (Just note that mycelium runners that grow near the surface of the glass rather than inside the substrate may appear to be a bit yellow. They are fine, so don't discard them.) However, if you do find a contaminated jar, carefully examine the adjacent jars. Remove all jars from the cooler, wash the outsides with antibacterial soap and spray with Lysol. Change the foil and wash out the

cooler with antibacterial soap and Lysol before replacing the jars.

4. Once you notice a primordium, it should mature into a mushroom ready for harvest in about a week. Use caution when harvesting. Take the mushroom by the base of the stalk with sterilized tweezers and wiggle it out.

5. Fill any holes with casing material. Continue to mist the casing and wait for the next flush!

TROUBLESHOOTING

This Tek is fairly self-explanatory when it comes to the problems you might encounter and how to deal with them. The only thing which is not addressed by the creator is the fact that some regions will not have an ambient temperature suitable for incubation. If you are using *P. cubensis*, this concern is minimized, but you may still need to adjust temperatures to fall within the 75-85-degree range. Aside from this, just make sure that you don't screw the lids on tightly during germination. This will prevent gas exchange and cause your mycelium to die.

Finally, **do not overwater!** With this method, ventilation is at a minimum. This is great to keep the jars humid. However, if there is too much water, **they will rot**. Err on the side of caution. And do not forget to move the bag (slowly) up and down over the jar a few times every day. This is the only thing that allows sufficient ventilation to the jar. You may also wish to use a 0.3% hydrogen peroxide solution for all watering, just to provide an additional measure against the risk of contamination.

COSTS AND CONSIDERATIONS

After reading the previous chapters and Teks, it will be evident to you that this is a low-tech and rather a sloppy method. However, it will do the job, and it's rather inexpensive. Even after buying the cooler, jars, substrate material, a sheet of plastic, and spore print, the cost should only come to about $60. If you buy a pressure cooker for the purpose of this method, the cost will be raised to about $100.

For subsequent batches, you will need to purchase only substrate material and spore print. In all honesty, a single spore print should be enough for at least two of these batches, and you can always make another from the first flush. Plus, if you have purchased the jars and pressure cooker for this batch, they will be helpful for a number of other methods as you continue your cultivation journey. So, really, if you choose to gather the materials for cultivation anyway, the cost for experimenting with this Tek along the way drops to close to nothing.

TEK FOR MAGIC TRUFFLES

This method is for the sclerotia-producing species like *P. mexicana* and *P. tampanensis*. The initial steps are the same as for previous Teks, also keeping strictly to sterile conditions:

- **Finding an initial culture**. For this method you can use a spore print, a spore syringe, mycelium water, colonized agar or colonized grain.
- **Preparing a substrate**. For these truffle species, it is best to use rye grass seeds or rye berries. With this basic mix the ratio is 10 parts seed to 5 parts water. You can also use wild bird seed, brown rice flour, or a coir/coffee/bran mix. (See the recipes below.)
- **Sterilizing the substrate**. You will use either quart sized Mason jars with lids and filters or grow bags. For the Mason jars, follow the instructions exactly as for the PF method (4 holes in lids, covering with aluminum, etc). Sterilize in a pressure cooker at 15 psi for 1 hour.
- **Inoculating the cooled substrate**. If you are using a syringe, then it is easy to use a sterilized needle through the syringe port in the bag. Otherwise follow the PF Tek for jars. Remember to shake the syringe to distribute the spores or mycelium. For spores, agar or grain, it will be necessary to open the bag or the jars to drop them in. This is best done in front of a flow hood or in a glovebox. Shake the bag and the jars to distribute the inoculate through the grain.

From here the process is different:

- **Germination and incubation** must happen in a dark place as for *cubensis,* but the temperature must be cooler, at about 70 to 77°F (21–25°C). Use an incubator if your ambient temperature is less than this. If it is higher, you might have to use some kind of cooling system, or wait for cooler weather.

- **Colonization** will take 2–4 weeks. You should shake the bag from time to time to loosen the substrate and allow the mycelium to spread.

- Once the bag has been fully colonized, most of the work is done, and from this point you just wait. Don't change any of the conditions as you do not want the mycelium to fruit.

- Leave the bag in the same dark place and at the same temperature, but do not shake again. This will stimulate the growth of what looks like little rocks on the mycelium. They will continue to grow for about 3–4 months. Be patient, this step takes longer than mushrooms but it is easier, and you will be able to harvest good-sized truffles. Remember to check and to mist to maintain humidity levels.

- **To harvest**, sterilize a spoon with alcohol and use it to scrape away the substrate from the sclerotia. Clean the truffles with a sterilized brush.

- **Store** in a paper bag in the refrigerator for a few weeks. For longer periods, dry the truffles by spreading out on brown paper in a warm room. You can use a fan to speed things up. Store in ziplock bags. Potency may diminish after 6 months.

Here is a bit more detail about some of these steps and 2 recipes for the substrata:

Recipe 1[8] for the substrate for *P. Mexicana*

- Heat water in a large pot (2.5 gallons or 9.5 liters)
- Brew a pot of strong coffee (about 2 quarts or 2 liters) and add to the hot water. Bring to the boil.
- Add 2 tsp of gypsum (calcium sulfate)
- Measure out 1 cup of rye for every quart Mason jar you intend to use.
- Rinse in a sieve to remove any debris.
- Add to the heated coffee/water and stir well. Turn off the stove.
- Leave for at least 4 hours and up to 24 hours.
- Bring back to the boil for 10–15 minutes.
- Turn off the stove and drain the water off the grains through a sieve.
- Leave the grains to get completely dry.
- Once they are dry, put about a cup into each Mason jar and cover with the lid and aluminum, as for the PF Tek. Sterilize for 90 minutes at 15 psi.
- Inoculate in the same way as for the PF Tek.

Recipe 2[9] for substrate for *P. Mexicana*

Ingredients

- 325g coir
- ½ cup used coffee grounds
- ½ cup wheat bran
- 1/8 cup gypsum

---

[8] Cultivation for Psilocybe Mexicana Mushrooms, Trufflemagic:/https://www.trufflemagic.com/proper-cultivation-for-psilocybe-mexicana-mushrooms/ (accessed January 23, 2019)

[9] Low-Maintenance Psilocybe Mexicana Fruiting Chamber Tek, Don Shadow:/https://www.shroomology.org/forums/topic/16079-low-maintenance-psilocybe-mexicana-fruiting-chamber-tek/ (accessed January 23, 2019)

- Calcium carbonate

Method

- Add water to coir to field capacity (cannot absorb any more)
- Mix other dry ingredients (except calcium carbonate) and mix with coir so that all coir is covered.
- Add calcium carbonate 1/8 teaspoon at a time until the mix reaches a pH of 7–8 (you may need a pH meter for this)
- Sterilize in Mason jar or grow bag. Seal the containers and use like any other bulk substrates.

Remember that these species will also fruit if you take the temperature up a bit and keep the humidity at about 95%. You might want to do this from time to time to collect spores or to clone very healthy specimens.

TEK FOR WOOD-LOVING SPECIES

Here's a Tek for *P. cyanescens*[10], one of the more potent mushrooms, also known as "blue meanies," "blue halos" and "wavy-capped psilocybe." Its natural habitat is on rotting wood. It is fairly widespread and can be found in the USA from California nearly to Alaska. It is also found throughout the UK and in many European countries including Spain, German, Italy and Sweden.

Germination and colonization

As for many psilocybe species, grain is a good growing medium for *P. cyanescens,* with rye being particularly well suited. The grain should be cooked and sterilized in exactly the same way as we described for P. mexicana and P. tampanensis in the previous Tek. (We also give all the steps for preparing grain in detail in the next chapter.) The inoculation technique is also exactly the same as for the P. Mexicana Tek.

What makes it different is that the colonized grain must be placed on a secondary substrate of alder chips that have been boiled for an hour to kill any contaminants. Mason jars with this mix of grain spawn and wood chips should be placed in a place where there is indirect sunlight and the temperature can be maintained at 73–77°F (23–25°C). This is a fairly narrow band, and will have to be managed with an incubator if necessary. Colonization will take 4–6 weeks.

Fruiting

To stimulate fruiting, cover the mycelium that has appeared on the surface of the substrate with a casing layer of

---

10 Psilocybe Cyanescens Cultivation Indoors (Trufflemagic):/https://www.trufflemagic.com/psilocybe-cyanescens/ (accessed January 23, 2019)

wet vermiculite, place the jars in the refrigerator and keep the temperature down to 43–47°F (6–8°C). Take the bottles out every two days or so to allow for some air to reach the mycelium. It might be a good idea to use the technique of a small plastic bag over the bottle that can just be moved slightly to create gentle air movement. Do this in front of your flow hood or in the glove box.

You should have fruiting bodies in 6 weeks.

INDOOR CULTIVATION: FINAL WORDS

There's nothing quite like the feeling you get when you harvest the first flush of mushrooms that you have cultivated yourself. Just like gardening brings you closer to your plants, mushroom cultivation gives you a greater appreciation for the mushroom. Soon, you'll want to expand your growing area and try out more complicated Teks. There are multiple ideas online and you can join one of the chat groups as people are generally very generous about sharing what they have learned.

We'd just ask you to remember the basic techniques you have learned here–and particularly all those that are to do with preventing contamination–and then adapt whatever you hear from others.

As a last step, I am going to give you a full chapter on propagating your own initial cultures–then you will not be dependent on anyone else and you can select, clone, and save your favorite species and the healthiest

CHAPTER 13. PROPAGATING YOUR OWN CULTURES

GETTING STARTED: IT STARTS WITH SPORES

MAKING SPORE PRINTS
MAKING SPORE SYRINGES
GERMINATING SPORES ON CARDBOARD
MYCELIUM SYRINGES

AGAR FOR GERMINATION

AGAR PLATES
RECIPES FOR AGAR PLATES
PROCEDURE FOR AGAR PLATES

GRAIN FOR GERMINATION

PREPARING THE GRAIN

INOCULATION

SPORES TO AGAR
AGAR TO AGAR
SPORES TO GRAIN
AGAR TO GRAIN
GRAIN TO GRAIN - EXPANDING THE SPAWN

CLONING

CLONING ON AGAR
CLONING ON CARDBOARD
CLONING ON GRAIN

LONG-TERM STORAGE

TROUBLESHOOTING FOR CONTAMINATION ON AGAR

CHAPTER 13. PROPAGATING YOUR OWN CULTURES

If you're a serious mushroom cultivator, knowing how to propagate and store cultures is an essential skill. The cultivation Teks we have described so far mostly assume that you will either buy or have someone give you the initial culture to work with. This could be a spore or mycelial syringe, or some spawn–mycelium that has colonized a growing medium or substrate.

In this chapter, we'll describe how you can propagate your own initial cultures and start the germination process. These can then be used to inoculate grain and other substrates and to grow the amount of spawn that you need.

Doing you own propagation can be by collecting your own spores and using them to make spore syringes or transferring them onto growing mediums. Or you might use a small piece of a healthy mushroom fruit to clone it and isolate that line.

To do all of this means knowing how to work with agar as a medium for germination. We'll give you some general tips about working with agar plates and some of the things to remember, no matter what recipe you are trying or technique you are using. The goal is to give you an overview, so that we won't have to repeat the same things for every new technique.

We also won't repeat all the steps about working in sterile conditions as they have been covered before. By now, you will have learned that not following the rules means that you will most likely lose your culture. At the end of the chapter, we'll give you a contamination troubleshooting checklist that covers the agar section. We hope that if you read it carefully, you'll know how to *avoid* contamination and you'll never need to troubleshoot.

This section is for advanced techniques, but they are built on the basic techniques described in detail in the Basic Tek chapter. So, we won't give detailed step-by-step instructions unless it's necessary. If you are in doubt about something, go back and check the basics. But, by now, you probably don't need to be told how to use a Mason jar or how to control the temperature for incubation.

GETTING STARTED: IT STARTS WITH SPORES

MAKING SPORE PRINTS

It's relatively easy to make a spore print. Essentially, you simply place a cap gill-side down on a surface and allow the spores to settle. However, there are a few important tips with regard to sterile culturing and storage. Here are the steps and then some tips:

Steps for making spore prints

1. Select the strongest and healthiest-looking mushroom. The cap must be open and quite flat.

2. Cut off the stem, as close to the cap as you can without touching the cap or the gills. Make sure your cut is straight so that the mushroom can stand on it.

3. Using a sharp knife, remove any bits of veil that remain.

4. Stand the mushroom on the cut-off stem on a flat surface covered with paper, glass or aluminum foil.

5. Cover the mushroom with a sterilized container (like a glass) to prevent air moving over it and to maintain its moisture.

6. Leave for 2–24 hours, depending on the humidity and the freshness of the mushroom. The spore will drop onto the surface, leaving the "print" pattern.

7. Seal the print. You can fold over and seal the paper or aluminum foil. If you have used glass, place another piece of glass on top of the first one and seal the edges.

8. Seal into plastic bags, mark with relevant information and store at room temperature in a place that is cool, dry and dark.

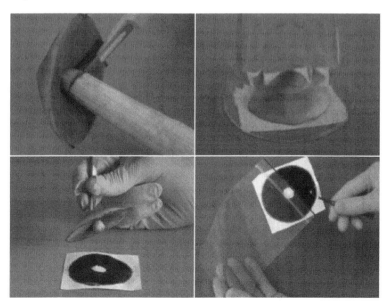

Special tips for making spore prints

The first tip is to keep everything as sterile as you can. This means using a sharp, sterilized knife, wiping down the collecting surface with alcohol and sterilizing the container you use to cover the mushroom.

The second is not to touch the gills or the bottom of the cap at any point as this might dislodge the spore prematurely or drop contaminants onto the surface. However, some people suggest putting one drop of water on the top of the cap just before you cover it as this stimulates the spores to drop.

Thirdly, choose your collection surface carefully. It must be flat. We prefer aluminum and glass on the surface because it is easy to wipe them down with alcohol, and it is easy to pick up the spores with an inoculation loop. But you can also use paper or even petri dishes, if they are the right size for the mushroom. Another useful method is to use an index card and a paper cup. Instead of cutting the stem off, use an index card covered with aluminum, with a hole in it. Put a paper cup under the card and slide the card up the stem. Then you have the cup to stand on as a firm surface.

Make sure that the pieces of paper or aluminum are long enough to fold over themselves and seal. Use sterilized tweezers to pick them up and place them into sealed bags. Make sure that the alcohol has dried before you put the mushroom onto the collection surface.

Fourthly, it is possible to make more than one print from a single cap. A tip is to use a pin used for sewing (the ones with the little plastic balls on the end). Sterilize the pin and push it through the top of the mushroom cap. You can then use tweezers to hold the pin head to pick up the mushroom and move it to a new spot.

And finally, if there are any signs of contamination, throw that print away and try to use the cap for a second print. Alternatively, throw the whole thing away rather than risk having everything else being contaminated too.

If you follow these steps, your spores should remain viable for several years.

MAKING SPORE SYRINGES

Once you have a spore print, one option is to make spore syringes. These are essential for the PF Tek method, and they can be used in some other methods as well. Here's what you will need:

Materials for making spore syringes

- Spore print
- Distilled water (approx 25 ml per syringe)
- Syringes and needles
- Alcohol lamp
- Inoculation loop or scalpel
- Mason jar with lid and filter disc
- Disinfectant
- Tweezers
- Dome hood and/or glove box

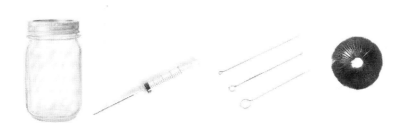

Special notes

What you are trying to do is move the spores into water in the syringes where they will hydrate for a few days before you use them to inoculate a new substrate. Keeping everything sterile along the way is critical, so it's best to do the spore transfer in front of a flow hood and/or in a glove box. A trick that we have seen is to add a few drops of dishwasher rinse aid to the distilled water. This stops the spores from clumping together and they also won't stick to the glass or the syringe. Remember that spores can only be seen under a microscope, so you might not see anything on the water.

Steps for making spore syringes

1. Pour distilled water into the Mason jar–approx 25ml per syringe that you plan to use.

2. Seal the jar with a lid and disc filter and sterilize the water and jar in your pressure cooker at 15 psi for 30 minutes.

3. Disinfect all surfaces where you will be working and allow to dry.

4. Allow the water to cool down completely and move the jar to your working surface. (Be patient here as hot water will kill the spores.)

5. Heat the inoculator loop or scalpel and the tweezers in the flame of the alcohol burner until they are red hot. Either wait a few minutes until they cool down or open the lid of the mason jar slightly and dip them into the cooled water. Close the jar.

6. Use sterilized tweezers to hold open the bag with the spore print in it. Don't move the print out of the bag.

7. Use the inoculator loop or scalpel to gather spores from the print. Close the bag after each pass.

8. Open the jar and swirl the loop in the water. Close the jar and repeat the process of collecting spores and putting them in the water a few times.

From this point you just have to follow the steps as the spores are too small for you to actually see them in the water.

9. Fill syringes with the water and spores from the jar. It's a good idea to fill and empty the syringes a few times each to make sure that the spores are dispersed evenly.

10. Replace the needle covers on the syringes and seal them into Ziploc bags. Label them clearly.

11. Store in a refrigerator. Note: You need to leave them for a day or two for the spores to hydrate but they will only remain viable for a month and a bit, so use them as soon as you can.

GERMINATING SPORES ON CARDBOARD

Cardboard is a remarkably effective medium for germinating mycelium. It retains moisture well and is wood based, so it is effective for a very wide range of species. If the outer layers are pulled off, there is often a corrugated section inside, and this is very good for air exchange. It seems quite resistant to contamination. Some people suggest soaking the cardboard in some kind of nutrient as a boost for the growth of mycelium, but others think that this just attracts potential contamination and soaking the cardboard in just water is good enough.

Spores are tiny, so we are going to use very small pieces of cardboard (one idea is to use a paper punch to press out little discs. Otherwise just cut very small squares of cardboard). You can use any thin piece of cardboard, such as that used for posters or the backs of notebooks.

For this method you are going to start the spores germinating on the cardboard–so mycelium will be forming before you put the discs into a growing medium like agar or grain. This means that you can use peroxide in them as it will not affect the mycelium.

You will be picking up spores from spore prints as you have done before, so keep in mind all the steps to keep everything sterile. Rather than using an inoculation loop, you will be using the sterilized tweezers to hold the piece of cardboard and running the edge through the spore print, and then you will drop it into a test tube with a malt-yeast-water solution and wait for the mycelium to germinate. Remember that spores are tiny and you may not be able to see them even if you have picked some up.

Preparing the materials

- Put cardboard pieces into a jar with a few ml of water.
- Put water or a nutrient mix into test tubes with lids (you can use the same malt and yeast mix that you use for agar plates or make a small amount - a teaspoon of malt, a pinch of yeast and about 100 ml water)
- Sterilize the jar with the cardboard and the test tubes in a pressure cooker for 15 minutes at 45 psi.

Picking up the spore

- Work in a well disinfected glove box or in front of a flow hood. Use an alcohol lamp to sterilize the tweezers between test tubes.
- Bring the jar of cardboard pieces and the test tube with the malt solution to the work top, together with the spore print in its plastic bag
- Follow the same steps as you did for picking up spore for spore syringes using the edge of the cardboard pieces to pick up the spores.
- Drop a few pieces of cardboard and spores into each test tube and seal the tubes with parafilm.

Germinating the mycelium

- Incubate at 75-85°F/24-30°C until you see that the mycelium has colonized the discs. This may take a day or two.
- Once the discs are colonized, you can transfer them to agar plates or directly into a substrate like grain.

MYCELIUM SYRINGES

Mycelium water is simply distilled water that has bits of mycelium in it. You can make it by cutting off a piece of colonized substrate and adding it to a jar of distilled water using the carefully sterile methods that we described for making spore water. Or...you can use this simple method using a colonized grain jar.

Steps for making mycelium water

1. Using a sterilized syringe, squirt distilled water into a colonized grain jar

2. Shake the jar back and forth a bit.

3. Pull the water back into the syringe.

4. Use this as soon as possible.

There you have it. Mycelium water can be used to inoculate substrate, just as you would use a spore solution. You may wish to mix a bit of peroxide into the mycelium water and swish it around before you use it. It will not harm the mycelium and will help to destroy any other contaminants that have made their way into the solution. You can use mycelium water to inoculate agar or grain, and one of the benefits is that it will work with mediums prepared with peroxide.

AGAR FOR GERMINATION

Once you have your spores or spore syringes, you want to have them germinate. Agar is the most popular medium to do this.

Agar is a jelly-like substance, obtained from red algae in seaweed. It is a polysaccharide, which means that it is a carbohydrate, made up of sugar molecules. It is widely used in microbiology labs as a culture medium. In fact, it was first noted in 1882 by a scientist working in the laboratory of Robert Koch (you may remember from an earlier section of this book that Robert Koch's laboratory was famous for understanding the role of steam, hot air and boiling for disinfection and sterilization).

Agar is a good medium because, although it provides some nutrient and a place for microorganisms and bacteria to grow, it is indigestible for them so they cannot eat it up and destroy it. It also has good gel stability. It melts only at 185°F (85°C) and remains solid even at around human body temperature of 98°F (37°C).

It generally is sold as a powder to be mixed with water, as you would with gelatin. It liquefies as it is heated. The liquid can be poured into petri dishes to cool, where it creates a semisolid layer.

Nutrients can be mixed with it to support the culture. A common choice is a mixture of malt and yeast extracts. However, pretty much any nutritional source can be combined with agar medium. It is also very versatile and can be stored for quite a while without a loss of viability, as long as you have maintained excellent sterile culture techniques.

Working with agar is best if you have a bit of experience, mainly because of the need for extremely sterile working conditions, but there are a number of advantages to it. Because the agar medium is flat and relatively dense, the culture will spread out two-dimensionally. This makes it easy to identify any contaminants. In addition, agar cultures can be cloned from the mycelium of a parent mushroom with desired characteristics. This allows the grower to isolate a single culture line. It can even be transferred from one plate to another, creating successive generations.

However, if you keep transferring them to plates that have the same medium, cultures will become less viable, grow weaker, and produce less fruit. The technical term for this loss of viability is senescence. You can strengthen them again by changing the composition of the medium. This seems to challenge the fungus to produce different sets of enzymes, essentially exercising it and encouraging it to stay healthy.

This is why you will need to learn a couple of recipes for your agar medium. This might mean just alternating with different types of grains. From time to time a bit of "shock therapy" is needed and then you can experiment with every type of nutritional source you can think of–and especially moving away from simple sugars to more complex ones. We've given you a recipe for this "revitalization" agar medium.

Another way to avoid senescence is by limiting the number of transfers made from one plate to the next. This is why we recommend you make a number of plates right at the start from your first healthy specimen and keep some of them in storage. Then you can start again when the current line starts looking a bit tired! You can use them to grow a new monoculture batch and re-isolate the strain from the mycelium. This will allow you to preserve and make use of a line for quite some time. You might have wondered why we added a Sharpie permanent marker to the list of essential equipment that you need. This is where it will come in–mark every culture you make clearly and include the number of times it has been transferred.

Remember, batches grown from spores will be genetically different from the parent mushroom, while those grown from the mycelium will be clones.

AGAR PLATES

An agar plate is a petri dish with agar and added nutrients, ready to be inoculated with spores or mycelium. You will use the plates to propagate cultures, germinate spores, clone mushroom fruitbodies and store cultures for long periods.

There are some tips to remember when you are working with agar plates:

- Mix and sterilize the medium in a bottle with a narrow neck, so that it is easy to pour into the petri dishes. Some people will use an old glass juice or whiskey bottle, plug it with some cotton and cover the top with aluminum. Use a wide funnel to pour the dry ingredients into the bottle.
- Sterilize prepared agar medium in a pressure pot for a maximum for about 30 minutes. Definitely don't go beyond 45 minutes to avoid caramelization of the sugars in the nutrients. Fungi won't grow on this.

- Agar foams when it is sterilized, so never fill the bottle more than 2/3. Never screw on a tight lid. Rather use cotton and aluminum to cover the mouth of the bottle.
- Agar will also boil over if it cools too quickly. Make sure that there is enough water in the pressure cooker to ensure that the water and agar cool at about the same rate.
- Read the instructions carefully for making the agar plate, as there are places where you must work while the material is still hot, sometimes when it is just warm, and other times when it must be completely cooled.
- Stand the bottle of agar in a shallow pot of hot water at ~150°F while you are working so that it doesn't solidify between pourings into the petri dishes.
- Work inside a glove box or under a laminar flow hood, sterilize all surfaces and equipment, wear gloves and even a surgical mask to prevent contamination.
- Stack the sterilized petri dishes on top of each other in stacks of about 10. To add the agar medium, start at the bottom of each stack. Lift the lid and the rest of the dishes up for just long enough to pour in the agar. Quickly replace the lid. Then move up to the next one.
- Seal the agar plates with parafilm if you are not going to use them immediately. Definitely seal them after you have inoculated them with the spores or the culture.

- When you are transferring spores or mycelium onto the prepared agar plates, open the lids of the petri dishes for as short a time as possible. Hold the lid directly over the dish as you work to prevent contamination. Do not lean over the plates or breathe directly on them. Start at the bottom of each stack as you did for pouring the agar.

- Inoculated petri dishes should be stored upside down after they have cooled and set, ie agar side up, lid side down. This gives you a good view of the growing culture and also keeps any possible moisture from condensation away from the culture.

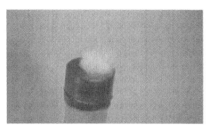

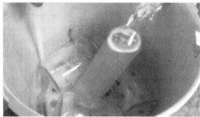

- Cover the stacks of dishes with the plastic or cardboard sleeves that the dishes came in or the aluminum that you used to wrap them for sterilization. Just make sure that there is sufficient air flow around them.

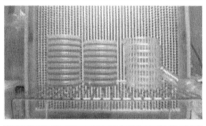

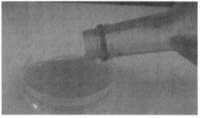

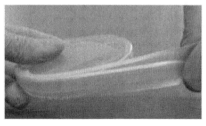

Photo Source: Freshcapmushrooms.com

RECIPES FOR AGAR PLATES

1. Malt Yeast Agar (MYA)

The MYA medium is very popular and can be used for all species of psilocybe. Some recipes are very simple–agar, malt, yeast and water. Others are a bit more complicated.

All of these recipes will give you about a liter of agar medium. This is enough for 20–30 standard sized petri dishes.

Recipe 1–the basic one

- 1L distilled water (it's best to heat it so the dry ingredients will mix better)
- 20g agar
- 20g light malt extract (not dark malt as this is caramelized and fungi will not grow on it)
- 2 g nutritional yeast

Some recipes say you can use tap water but be careful of chlorine levels.

Some people want some additional nutrition and add 0.1g of potassium dibasic (K_2HPO) and 0.1g calcium carbonate ($CaCO_3$) (oyster shell will work).

Recipe 2 (can also be used for wood-loving species)
(Thanks to Nicholas and Ogamé[11] for this recipe)

- 1L tap water
- 22g agar

---

[11] PSILOCYBIN MUSHROOM HANDBOOK: EASY INDOOR & OUTDOOR CULTIVATION (2006) BY L. G. NICHOLAS, KERRY OGAMÉ.

- 12g light malt extract
- 5g hardwood sawdust or wood fuel pellets
- 1g yeast extract
- ¼ tsp organic grain flour (rotate between millet, rye, cornmeal, oats, rice, amaranth, wheat, or any other starch or sugar)
- 8ml of 3% hydrogen peroxide (Optional, to be used only for agar cultures intended for mycelial cultures. **Reminder: Hydrogen peroxide will kill spore inoculations!**)

Potato Dextrose Agar

Some people use this instead of the MYA. Others use it in rotation with MYA to prevent senescence.

- 1L broth from boiling 250 grams sliced unpeeled potatoes in 1.2L water for 30 minutes, then straining through cheesecloth or muslin. (You can use 10 g of instant potato flakes instead)
- 20g agar
- 10g dextrose (glucose), or 10 ml honey or corn syrup
- 1.5 - 2g gram brewer's yeast or yeast-extract (optional)
- Add the mixed dry ingredients to the broth and boil gently until the solution is clear (add water to keep it at 1L).

You can pour this mixture directly into petri dishes and then sterilize them, or sterilize in a bottle and then pour into petri dishes, as for the other recipes.

PROCEDURE FOR AGAR PLATES

We've given a few recipes, but the method remains the same:

1. Combine all dry ingredients in a bottle, followed by the water. The jar should be 1.5 to 2 times the volume of the contents. This will prevent it from boiling over. Plug the opening with cotton and cover with aluminum.

2. Sterilize the bottle and its contents in the pressure cooker at 15psi for 30–45 minutes (no longer, so sugars do not caramelize). This will also liquefy the agar. Also wrap any other equipment you are using in aluminum and sterilize at the same time. If you are using glass and not pre-packed and pre-sterilized petri dishes, sterilize them too. Stack about 10 of them together with their lids and wrap in aluminum.

3. Allow the cooker and the bottle to cool slightly, but it must remain warm enough for the agar to still be liquid. Handle everything carefully, as surfaces will be hot! Move bottle and sterilized equipment to the previously sterilized glove box or flow hood area.

4. If you are adding hydrogen peroxide, now is the time to do it–but let the agar cool a bit more first so you can handle the bottle comfortably. Add the peroxide with a pipette and swirl it around gently to mix but not add bubbles.

5. Pour agar into the stacks of petri dishes, working from the bottom of each stack and leaving each dish open for as short a time as possible, as described earlier.

6. Seal each dish with parafilm. Cover the stacks of plates with the original plastic sleeves or the aluminum foil that originally covered them.

7. Once they have thoroughly cooled, turn the dishes upside down and store them until you need them.

GRAIN FOR GERMINATION

The purpose of propagating your own cultures is to use them to grow mushroom spawn, which is the combination of mycelium and substrate. This substrate is mostly grain-based, often mixed with vermiculite, with added calcium carbonate and calcium sulfate. As a rule of thumb, you will use a ¼ teaspoon of each to every cup of dry grain. You will use a little more for large quantities–so for spawn bags use about 2 teaspoons of each.

The type of grain that you will use depends on the species of mushroom you are working with. *P.cubensis* is pretty easy to please, but some of the others are pickier. Check the recipes that are given for different Teks for ideas on what to use. Rye, wheat, brown rice, wild bird seed and even popcorn are popular. Rye is particularly good because it absorbs water so well.

However, the methods used are generally the same, and so are the principles: grain must be properly prepared and sterilized and must have the right moisture content if you want successful mycelial growth.

Excess moisture should be avoided in larger containers. The grain will not colonize quickly enough to absorb it, so it will lead to contamination. Because of this, large volumes of substrate require more gypsum and calcium carbonate. You also need more hydrogen peroxide to contend with the greater risk of contamination. So you will use about 80ml per bag compared to just 6ml in a mason jar!

Avoid overcooking the grain, as the kernels might crack open–this increases the risk of contamination. This is why long soaking is recommended rather than long boiling. Rinse cooked grain well to remove some of the starchy stickiness and drain it completely before loading the bags. You'll want the grain almost dry to the touch.

Deciding how much to prepare can be tricky. Remember that you will eventually want your mason jar or spawn bag ⅔ to ¾ full. The grain will more or less double in volume when cooked. So, the tip is to use one of your jars and measure out one jar of dry grain for every 3 jars that you will be using. Add a little for good measure! For spawn bags, use 7–10 cups of dry grain which will swell up to 18 to 25 cups.

PREPARING THE GRAIN

The steps are quite simple:

1. Rinse the grains to remove debris and some surface starch. Keep rinsing till the water runs clear.

2. Cover with water and cook for about 10–15 minutes, then turn off the heat and allow standing for 12–24 hours. Some recipes reverse this–first soak for 12–24 hours and then cook for 10–15 minutes. Others boil at the start, then soak , then boil again for a short while. The heat at the end helps with drying the grain as a lot of moisture will steam off. The long period of soaking will cause many possible contaminants to sprout, and they will then be more easily killed in the pressure pot.

3. Drain well through a sieve or colander. Shake a few times to help the steam to escape. If the grains are still sticky, rinse a few times in clean water. Then spread out

on a towel or screen to dry out. You want the grain to be nearly dry to the touch, with each kernel separate, but soft inside.

4. Load grain and the appropriate amounts of calcium carbonate and calcium sulfate into mason jars or spawn bags, shake to disperse and sterilize at 15 psi. Bottles are usually for 90 minutes. Large spawn bags can be up to 2.5 hours.

Remember the rules for mason jars, with holes in the lids, breathable filters and covering with aluminum to prevent water from getting into the bottles.

The trick with spawn bags is to add the grain, press out any air, then fold the top of the bag to the side opposite the filter patch. Stack into the pressure cooker with the folds down and the patches facing up, and all of them exposed–i.e. don't pack bags on top of each other to block the patches. You are going to add 80ml peroxide to each bag after it is sterilized, so remember to put the measuring beaker, wrapped in foil, into the pressure cooker at the same time.

5. Allow the bottles or bags to cool down in the pressure cooker. Then move them to a sterilized work surface in front of your flow hood or in a glove box. Inspect each one and discard if the kernels have split or are glued together and can't be separated by shaking.

6. Add the peroxide to each container (6 ml for a bottle, 80ml for a bag) and shake to disperse.

Your grain is now ready for inoculation.

INOCULATION

Once you have spores or mycelium available you can use it to inoculate various forms of growing mediums to propagate mycelium and, eventually, mushroom fruit bodies. This includes inoculating agar plates, cardboard and grain, and then going on to expand the amount of spawn that you have. The steps to keep everything as sterile as possible are of particular importance at the inoculation stage.

After inoculation, keep the growing medium in a draft-free, dark area and keep the temperature at between 75 and 85°F/24-30°C to incubate until the mycelium has taken hold.

Mycelium that has grown on agar plates can be kept for as long as you want – keep it in the refrigerator. However, if you have used grain it is best to use it within a week to ten days as it will lose its strength after this.

SPORES TO AGAR

There are two methods – either using spores directly from a spore print or using a spore syringe. Both methods will provide a large number of spores into your medium.

VERY IMPORTANT: When you are using spores never use agar dishes that have peroxide added to them as this will kill the spores.

Using spore prints

To use spore prints to transfer spores onto agar medium, follow the same instructions as you would for creating spore syringes (see instructions earlier in this chapter). The only difference is that the spore-laden inoculation loop is swiped in an S-shape through the agar instead of through water. Close the dish and seal with parafilm. Store upside down after a day or two.

Using a spore or mycelium syringe

You can also use a spore or mycelium syringe. Lift the lid of the petri dish and inject about 1ml of solution into the agar at three or four points around the dish. Replace lid and allow the culture to develop for a day or two before storing upside down. If you are using a mycelium syringe, you can use agar with peroxide in it.

Using spore from cardboard

For this method, the spores started germinating on little cardboard discs–so mycelium will be forming before you put the discs onto the agar. This means that you can use agar plates that have peroxide in them as it will not affect the mycelium.

Follow the instructions given earlier in this chapter to colonize the discs in test tubes. Once the discs are colonized, transfer a few from each test tube to individual peroxide-containing agar plates. Follow the same procedure as for agar to agar transfer below, to avoid contamination. Use sterilized tweezers instead of a scalpel to move the cardboard onto the agar. Incubate the plates until you are ready to use them.

AGAR TO AGAR

In this technique, you are simply going to take a small piece of colonized agar from one plate and place it face down in a new agar plate. Both plates should have peroxide in them. The mycelium will then have peroxide-containing agar on both sides. This will destroy any contaminants on the mycelium and will also promote fast new growth.

Remember that if you have used spores to start the culture on agar, you are likely to have hundreds of different strains in the same plate (remember the section on the biology of mushrooms?) In some cases there will be so many strains growing on top of each other that you will not be able to decide on a strong one to select. You might have to make several agar-to-agar transfers of small pieces until you can start to isolate just a few strains. Then you can select the strongest looking ones to continue the agar to agar inoculation to eventually grow out the best fruiting strains. Look for dense growth and avoid anything wispy or slow-growing.

Once you have isolated the strain that you want, remember to keep some in storage in the refrigerator so that you can always go back to grow it out again. Also, to avoid contamination, cut the pieces you are going to use at least 1 cm away from the edge of the dish and also away from the original tissue.

Procedure

1. It is important to work quite quickly, using a glove box or laminar flow hood and, of course, sterilizing everything as you go. Wear gloves and a mask.

2. Remove the parafilm from the dish holding the culture and from the fresh petri dish(es) and place them side by side in front of the hood. Put the culture plate in front of your working hand, and the fresh plate(s) on the opposite side.

3. Keep the alcohol lamp burning all the time as you will be sterilizing the scalpel between each transfer.

4. Heat the blade of the scalpel in the alcohol lamp until it is red-hot. Quickly lift the lid of the new dish and dip the blade into the agar to cool it. Keep your hand on the back half of the lid, and downstream from the plate. Make sure that you do not touch the edge of the plate with your hand. Replace the lid.

4. Lift the lid of the culture plate slightly and cut as many ½-1cm wedges or squares as needed.

5. Remove the lid of the culture plate and slide the lid of the clean plate to the side. Pick up a portion of colonized agar with the tip of your scalpel and place it face down in the center of the new plate. Replace the new lid. Make sure that the colonized piece stays in the airflow and upstream of the new plates. Repeat until all plates contain mycelium-impregnated agar. Replace the lid of the original culture.

Photo Source: Freshcapmushrooms.com

6. Seal with parafilm and mark all plates. The inoculated agar will stick to the fresh agar so you can store them upside down immediately.

7. Incubate, either in an incubator or at room temperature (if your room temperature is between 75 and 85°F/24-30°C) until the mycelium covers the new plates.

One very interesting variation on this technique is to place the inoculated agar not on the top of the agar in the new plate, but *underneath*. The reason for doing this is to avoid the slow build-up and spread of contamination when mycelium is repeatedly moved from plate to plate. You can stop this by implementing the changed method after every few transfers.

If the mycelium is at the bottom of the agar, it is forced to grow upwards through the peroxide-containing agar and any contaminants are left in the bottom of the dish.

Procedure:

- The steps are similar to those given above.

- At step 2, the fresh petri dish is turned upside down onto its lid. The lid is then loosened, and the dish is lifted from one side. Use a flamed scalpel to ease the agar out of the dish and onto the lid. (If it breaks, then you will know to add more agar to your mix next time.)
- Close the dish again, until step 5.
- At step 5, lift the dish and place the culture face-down on the exposed underside of the fresh agar. Close the dish and turn it right side up. If necessary, use a flamed scalpel to nudge the agar back into it old position in the dish, but now sitting on top of the piece of mycelium.

SPORES TO GRAIN

Several methods for inoculating grain were given in the Tek chapter. All of those examples used spores, spore syringes or mycelial syringes that you had to acquire from elsewhere. Now that you know how to make your own spore prints and syringes, you can follow the instructions given in the Teks to inoculate grain substrates.

However, the Beginner Teks did not tell you how to transfer agar cultures onto your grain mix.

AGAR TO GRAIN

As for the agar-to-agar method, you use a sterilized scalpel to cut the colonized agar culture into ½ to 1cm squares or wedges. You will be transferring them to sterilized grain, usually in mason jars., rather than to agar plates. As a guide to size, you should be able to inoculate 6 jars from one agar plate. If you are going to add 2 or 3 pieces per jar, cut the pieces a bit smaller.

All the steps to avoid contamination remain the same. Be especially careful to wipe down all the surfaces of the agar plate with alcohol. This is a time to work in front of a laminar flow hood or at least a glove box. Re-sterilize your scalpel between jars. Leave the lids of the jars open for as short a time as possible – someone has suggested 2 seconds at most. It's a good idea to add hydrogen peroxide to each jar of grain before you add the agar.

The process is quite simple:

1. Prepare the grain in mason jars as described in the previous section of this chapter.
2. Open the lid just a crack and quickly put at least two or (preferably) three wedges or squares of colonized agar into each jar. Using more pieces leads to faster colonization and less likelihood of contamination. Try to spear all the pieces of agar at the same time so that you have to open the jar only once. Push the tip of the scalpel into the agar if the pieces don't want to come off. Another trick is to tip the jars slightly so that the grain is lying at an angle. The agar then runs down the slope and when you start to shake the jar the agar is already at a greater depth in the grain and is easier to cover.
3. Then close the lids of the jars and gently shake the containers so that the grain covers the mycelium and the grain is level. You want to increase the number and spacing of inoculation points, but you don't want to shake the mycelium off the agar.
4. Label the jars and incubate them as described earlier. Remember to loosen the lids slightly to allow for gas exchange, so the mycelium doesn't die.

Don't shake the containers again until you can see that the mycelium has started to spread. Shake after about a week and then again when about 50% of the grain has been colonized. This breaks up the mycelium and spreads it through the substrate.

When the jar is white and all the grains have been covered by mycelium (usually 1 – 3 weeks), it's ready to be moved into a fruiting chamber– or you can expand it by adding it to other jars or into spawn bags and starting the process again.

Photo Source: Freshcapmushrooms.com

Just as a note: it is not a good idea to use agar cultures in large containers or spawn bags of grain. The pieces are too small and will take too long to colonize the space. The risk of contamination then grows.

You can make as much spawn as you need. One jar of spawn will make another 10 jars or about 4 spawn bags (about 1 cup per bag).

Shake the fully colonized bottle or bag to loosen the spawn. Leave it for about two days for the mycelium to start spreading again. This is an important step. You want to see that the mycelium starts growing quickly again and that there is no contamination.

Wipe the colonized bottle down thoroughly with alcohol – be particularly careful to wipe around the bottom of the screw section of the lid. To prevent contamination, work in your glove box or in front of the flow hood. Use gloves.

Procedure

- Prepare the grain in the jars or bags as described in the previous section of this chapter. Remember to add hydrogen peroxide (6ml per jar, 80ml per bag). It's also really important to make sure that your grain is as dry as possible. Too much moisture in a bag is a sure place for contamination to start.
- Shake the bottle of colonized spawn to break it up, then tip about a cup of spawn into each spawn bag. Do this one bag at a time, closing the flap each time. For jars, remember that one jar is enough for 10 new ones.
- Seal the lids of the jars. Seal each bag with an impulse sealer. Do about 3 seals per bag, about 2 cm apart to make sure it doesn't come open.

- Shake the bags and bottles thoroughly to disperse the mycelium, label them and incubate under the usual conditions.
- Check regularly and break up and disperse the mycelium once it starts to take hold. You can shake the bottles and manipulate the bag rather than shaking it.

Remember that growing mycelial cultures generate heat. Larger containers can produce quite a bit of heat, so you'll want to be careful not to allow the culture to overheat while it's incubating. Keep the bags in a cooler space, in temperatures that range from 65 to 75°F/18-24°C. Make sure that the bags do not touch one another. Keep about 4" between them so that air can circulate. If necessary, you can use a fan to help dissipate heat.

Although, theoretically, you could continue expanding spawn like this forever, 3 times is usually the limit as the risk of contamination will grow with each repeat.

CLONING

Cloning is one of the most exciting things we can do with mushroom cultivation, and, given the versatility of fungi, it's easier than you might imagine. This is a straight tissue transfer from a fruiting body and it's called cloning because the resulting culture will be genetically identical with the parent mushroom. The only difficult part about this is making sure that you work in a sterile environment and don't transfer any contaminant from the mushroom fruit to the agar.

CLONING ON AGAR

On agar it is really easy. All you have to do is place a small internal piece of a stipe on a peroxide agar plate. Literally. That's it. Incubate the plate, and the stem will revert to mycelium and culture the plate.

Photo Source: Freshcapmushrooms.com

Directions

- Work in sterilized conditions as usual and sterilize all equipment.
- Use agar plates that have peroxide in them.
- Wipe down the mushroom with an alcohol-soaked swab, hold it at the base and use a scalpel to cut lengthwise up the stem and into the cap. Otherwise, you can press it to split it open. You want to expose the inside.
- Cut 2–7mm squares or wedges of mycelium from the inside section–not from any of the external parts as they may be contaminated.
- Pick up the pieces with the tip of the scalpel and drop one piece onto the center of each agar plate, cover it with agar, seal the dish and incubate. Remember to sterilize the scalpel between dishes.
- Turn the dishes upside down once the mycelium has begun growing into the agar.

CLONING ON CARDBOARD

Cardboard can be used very effectively for germinating mycelium directly from mushroom tissues.

- Cut strips of cardboard about 2–3cm wide and long enough to fit onto the bottom of the mason jars. You will need 2 per jar. Moisten the cardboard and add all the strips of cardboard into one Mason jar. You can add a bit of extra water into the jar to make sure that the cardboard is wet enough.

- Sterilize this jar together with the clean jars you are going to use for about 45 minutes at 15 psi. Allow them to cool in the pressure cooker, and then move to your sterilized work space.
- Prepare pieces of mushroom tissue as you did for the agar above.
- Open the jar with the cardboard, pick up a piece of cardboard, and place it into a new jar. Pick up a piece of tissue to place onto the cardboard. Then place a second piece of cardboard on top of the tissue. Press down with the tweezers to make sure everything is in contact with everything else. Sterilize the tweezers between each step. Add a bit of the sterilized water if the cardboard is not wet enough. Seal the jar.
- Repeat until you have done all of the jars.
- Allow to incubate. Add a bit of water if the cardboard seems to be getting dry.

Once the cardboard has colonized, you can move pieces directly to agar or to a grain substrate to continue the germination.

One technique that I saw added popcorn to the jar with the cardboard, allowed that to colonize, then added water and used it to make spore syringes.

CLONING ON GRAIN

Several people have asked whether you could colonize grain directly with a tissue sample. This is theoretically possible, but the reason we don't recommend is that the risk of contamination is too high. Grain substrate is full of nutrients and all of them could harbor some contaminant. Agar and cardboard are low in nutrients and the risk is therefore reduced.

Cloning is an incredibly simple way to isolate a culture line. All you have to do is find a particularly impressive fruiting body and follow the processes we have provided. Next thing you know, you'll have a single culture that you can use to colonize substrate and begin growing flushes. To find a desirable culture, look for specimens that fruit densely and early and that produce large fruits with a healthy appearance. This will increase the likelihood that the resulting culture provides consistent, abundant fruiting.

Long-term Storage

When you become more expert at identifying and propagating good strains you will want to make sure that you can duplicate them. So, you want to keep a "master" of each good strain that you can subculture whenever you want to. You also want to make sure that you always have a stock of cultures in case something happens to your current batches or they are showing signs of senescence. This is why we keep emphasizing the importance of properly labeling every inoculated agar plate.

Germinated cultures can be stored for a surprisingly long time. Cultures in agar can be stored in petri dishes or test tubes in a refrigerator for years. To get them growing again, you only have to take them out, let them get to room temperature for about 48 hours and transfer them to new dishes. Then they can go back into the refrigerator again if you like. It's a good idea to "refresh" them like this every year or two.

Troubleshooting for Contamination on Agar

As is emphasized earlier, contamination is your greatest challenge in mushroom cultivation. You'll come across it from time to time, no matter how careful you are. I recommend that you go back and re-read the section on keeping your workplace sterile in Chapter 10.

It's easy to spot contamination on agar plates. If the agar becomes cloudy or you see some color change, assume that there is contamination. Fungal contamination is fuzzy, with filamentous or hair-like growths. It often occurs along the edges of an agar plate. Bacterial contamination will look slimy, shiny, and translucent. The colors will tend to be yellow, pink or white. If you see it, dispose of the plate.

On grain, you will see similar signs of contamination. There might also be a sour smell like rotten apples–you will be able to check this at the filter holes. Another sign of contamination in grains is if the mycelium is slow to retake, or doesn't regrow, after you have shaken the bottles or bags.

If you absolutely must try to save an agar plate, then remove the uncontaminated section of the culture and transfer it to a fresh plate. Don't try to cut away the contaminant and leave the culture on the same plate. Even if you do move to a new plate you might find some mold spores have remained and you may have to change plates several times before you have a clean culture.

It really is best to simply throw away any contaminated material. Move it away from other uncontaminated material as quickly as possible, thoroughly wash and sterilize any containers that you are going to use again, shower yourself and put on clean clothes before you go back into your working area.

Here is a troubleshooting checklist for agar–there are obviously many ways that you can introduce contamination here! We've also given a few signs that may look like contamination but actually have another cause.

Symptom	Probable cause	Remedy
Plates are contaminated before inoculation	Petri dishes not sterilized properly	Follow sterile working rules
	Sterile rules not followed when pouring solution into petri dishes	
	Not enough hydrogen peroxide in solution	
Contamination on the edge of the plate	Unsterile air pulled in when the plate cooled	Let the agar cool enough before pouring. Cover stacks of petri dishes with plastic or cardboard tubes or the aluminum you used to sterilize them.
Contamination at the inoculation point	Either the culture or one of your tools was not sterile: the scalpel, the syringe or the inoculation loop	Heat tools until they are red hot before using them (cool by dipping into clean agar before using) Examine the culture carefully before transfers.

Slimy, shiny patches	Bacterial colonies. They thrive in moisture, so they are often introduced from condensation on the lids during cooling.	Let the agar cool enough before pouring. Allow the dish to cool slowly, and place it immediately in the plastic or cardboard sleeve. Make sure that there is air circulation around the tube. Store agar-side up once it has set and the mycelium has started to grow.
	Edges of the petri dishes not properly sealed	Seal with parafilm
Contamination in some plates after transfer, but not all of them	Contamination from the air. Scalpel not properly sterilized between plates	Lift the lids of the dishes as little and for as short a time as possible. Work beneath a flow hood or inside a glove box Use plates that have had peroxide added Sterilize scalpel after each transfer
	Transfers taken from the edges of the dish or from the original plug of inoculum in the center of the dish	Avoid the centre and 1cm from the edge of the dish when taking transfers

Contamination starting after a few plate to plate transfers of the same batch	Contamination from the air from frequent moves, leading to slow build-up of contamination	Be super vigilant about sterilization techniques. Try transferring culture to the bottom of the new agar medium, instead of the top. Discard this batch and start again with the "master" you have stored in the refrigerator
Mycelium slows or dies	Primary sign of poor health and/or contamination.	Discard.
	Agar has dried out, either because there is not enough free air flow or there is not enough agar in plate Agar has been stored in the freezer (this is a no-no unless you are an expert in liquid nitrogen techniques)	Never incubate or store agar cultures in a completely sealed system – use parafilm or cotton for plugs or caps. Have a fan in the refrigerator Use 14ml of agar medium instead of the standard 10 ml per plate
	Sugars in the agar medium have caramelized and mycelium will not grow on this (usually for Malt Yeast Agar mediums)	Sterilize the bottle and its contents in the pressure cooker at 15psi for 30–45 minutes (no longer, so sugars do not caramelize)

Some mycelial growth looks different from the rest or grows at a different rate.	This may be sectoring rather than contamination and is a form of genetic change. It is often on the leading edge of the growth. Some may be fluffy arial growth and some may be brownish. It is likely to affect the productivity of the culture.	Rather select the mycelium that is uniform to ensure reliable growth

I really hope all of this information helps and that you have a trouble-free and fun time with your mushroom cultivation!

PART IV
GENERAL INFORMATION

CHAPTER 14. LEGALITY

Psilocybin and psilocin have been declared Schedule I drugs by the United Nations in the 1971 Convention on Controlled Substances. They are highly controlled and possession, creation, transport, and sales carry heavy penalties. However, these legislations do not address psilocybin mushrooms or any preparations made from them. Furthermore, they do not address cultivation. So, as far as United Nations regulations go, possession, cultivation, and consumption of psilocybin mushrooms is fair game.

Before you jump for joy, hold on for a moment. While the UN doesn't have much to say about it, every country has its own regulations. At this point, cultivation of psilocybin mushrooms is only legal in **Austria, Brazil, the British Virgin Islands, Bulgaria, Jamaica, and the Netherlands**. While cultivation is illegal in the U.S., grow kits and spores are legal in most states. In some states, notably Idaho and Georgia, the spores are illegal both to sell and to possess. In Canada and South Africa, cultivation is illegal, but growing kits and spores are legal. Similarly, in Russia and Japan, cultivation is illegal, but spores are legal. However, growing kits are to be avoided in both countries.

There are some places where psilocybin mushroom cultivation is a bit of a grey area. In Austria, for example, they are legal only if they are not grown to be used as drugs. In the Czech Republic, Italy, Portugal, and Spain, cultivation is illegal but decriminalized. In Spain, the consumption of mushrooms in a private space has also been decriminalized. Remember, decriminalized does not mean legal. It is still illegal, but does not carry extreme penalties.

Finally, there are some countries in which cultivation is illegal, but this law is not enforced. These countries include Thailand, Laos, and India. Also, while indoor cultivation is illegal in Mexico, some outdoor beds might skate the edge of the law if they are "grown in the wild." With Mexico, this has to do with the use of psilocybin mushrooms in local tribal culture.

As mentioned in the introduction, this book is not intended in any way to promote cultivation in countries where it is illegal. It is a great shame that these countries have passed these legislations, and my sincere hope is that they will be changed in the near future. However, in the meantime, it is wise to honor the laws of the countries we live in.

APPENDIX: MAGIC MUSHROOM RECIPES

MAGIC MUSHOOM RECIPES

TEAS

LEMON OR LIME SHOT

MEALS

CHOCOLATE TRUFFLES

SOME FINAL THOUGHTS ON CONSUMPTION

APPENDIX: MAGIC MUSHROOM RECIPES

TEAS

For all tea recipes, chop up or crush the mushrooms or truffles, both fresh and dry. This increases the surface area exposed to the water. You can keep them in a bag and crush them with your hands or use a grinder.

Basic tea

Add the mushrooms to a pot of boiled water (after it has cooled slightly) and then allow it to simmer gently for 30 minutes to an hour. Let it stand for 15 minutes and then drink. You can strain it or drink it with all the pieces in it.

Some recipes say that you should add the mushrooms to the water and wait for them to sink to the bottom, to know that the tea is ready. Stirring speeds this up. You can also pour everything into a mason jar, close the lid and shake it from time to time to encourage the pieces to fall to the bottom.

Alternatively, add the pieces to a tea infuser and pour the boiled water over them. Let it steep for about 15 minutes, stirring occasionally. Strain into another cup and drink.

You can use the strained bits for a second time for another cup if you want to.

Ginger and licorice tea

Add some chopped dried licorice (or a licorice flavored tea bag) to the chopped mushrooms. After you add the water, add a small amount of ginger (fresh is best, or about half a teaspoon of ginger powder). When it has steeped for long enough, top it

up with some fresh orange juice. This is a great tasting drink–
the licorice combines well with the taste of mushrooms and the
ginger and orange will help with any nausea you may feel.

LEMON OR LIME SHOT

As explained earlier, lemon or lime juice will hasten the
breakdown of psilocybin into psilocin and both hasten and
strengthen the effect.

Grind your mushrooms into as fine a powder as possible
and place into a small glass. Cover with freshly squeezed juice.
Stir every 5 minutes or so. After about 20 minutes, but no
longer than an hour, drink it down in one shot. Rinse the glass
with a bit of water to get the last of the powder. Then wait for
the action!

MEALS

We've given you a few ideas for light meals, a main meal
and a dessert. Also, you can use any of your favorite recipes
and replace the ordinary mushrooms with the magic variety.
Just take note of how much you are adding, and be very careful
of portion sizes.

Light meals or snacks
Mini quiches

A quiche is really simple. We recommend minis rather
than a large pie, so that you have a better idea of how much
mushroom you have in each serving.

The problem you may have is that mushrooms are very
watery, and you don't want a soggy quiche. So if you are
rehydrating your mushrooms, use only ½ cup of warmed milk
to 4g of dried mushrooms, and use whatever milk remains in

the egg mix later. Also, when you precook the veggies, the mushrooms will release a lot of moisture. Don't waste any that remains in the pan. Replace some of the milk in the egg mix with this liquid. You might have to add an extra egg if you are adding more than about quarter of a cup of mushroom liquid.

Use frozen pastry to line muffin pans, cover with wax paper and beans (for weight), and pre-bake for about 15 minutes. Allow to cool slightly, then remove the beans and the paper, prick the bottom of the shells with a fork (to release air) and put back into the oven for about 10 minutes until golden. (Or you can buy ready cooked pastry shells.)

Ingredients:

You can use any mushroom quiche recipes. Remember it is just

- Grated cheese, on the base of the baked pastry shell (Gruyère or Bergeron are good, but you can use any hard cheese)–about 1½ cups for 12 mini quiches.
- Vegetables of some sort, stir fried for a short while and as dry as possible (You can do mushrooms on their own; or kale/spinach, red onion and mushroom are a good combination). Put this on top of the grated cheese.
- An egg, cream and milk mix. (The ratio is ½ cup of cream, ½ cup milk and 3 eggs–start with the eggs in the measuring jug and make sure that the total is to the 1½ cup mark). Beat really well till frothy. Add salt and pepper and a pinch of nutmeg, pour over the veggies and you're good to go.
- Bake at a low temperature (325 F or 160 C) until the mixture sets.

You can freeze them, so it's OK to make a big batch!

Ideas for the main course

Chili gone Psily

Ingredients

Here's a very simple chili recipe, but you might have your favorite with a few more ingredients (mine adds paprika, cumin and marjoram, with sour cream to serve).

- 500g chopped beef (hamburger)
- 2 cans chopped tomatoes
- 1 onion, finely chopped
- 2 cloves garlic, crushed
- 1 tsp oil
- 1 stock cube crumbled or 2 teaspoons stock powder
- 1 can red kidney beans
- 1 heaped tsp HOT chili powder or 1 Tbsp mild chili powder
- 1 tsp sugar (or a thumb-nail size piece of dark chocolate–this balances out the acidity of the tomatoes and adds body and color)
- Enough freshly cooked rice (long grain), for a small helping for each person.
- Fresh mushrooms, cut up into very small pieces–weigh out a portion for each person.

Method

1. Heat oil in a pan or wok and sauté the onions till soft. Add the garlic and the chili powder and cook on

medium heat for about 5 minutes. Remove from the pan.

2. Turn up the heat. Add the ground beef and brown it. Keep the heat on fairly high so that the meat browns and doesn't stew. Keep stirring so it doesn't burn.

3. Add back the onions, both cans of tomatoes, the sugar (or chocolate) and the stock powder. You might add about 300 ml water.

4. Bring to a simmer and then reduce the heat to very low, cover with a lid and allow to simmer for about 20 minutes.

5. Keep checking and stirring and add a bit of water if it seems to be drying out.

6. Drain and rinse the can of beans and add to the pot. Bring to the boil again, and then cook gently for about 10 minutes, this time without the lid. Again, add a few tablespoons of water if it is not looking soft and juicy.

7. Taste and add salt and pepper if needed. This dish takes more seasoning than you may expect.

8. Replace the lid, turn off the heat and leave it to stand for 10 minutes for all the flavors to mingle.

9. While the chili is cooking, cut up the mushrooms into very small pieces and weigh out a portion for each person.

To serve:

10. Dish up the chili for each person into individual bowls and mix in their portion of mushrooms. Serve with the rice (and sour cream if you like it).

CHOCOLATE TRUFFLES

Not so simple, but very delicious are **chocolate truffles**. This recipe is courtesy of a fellow-traveler and taken from myctopia[12]. She has recommended Kaluha (a rum and coffee liqueur) and mint, but you can use whatever your favorite flavors are. She used rainbow sprinkles as a decoration (she says she associates them with magic!) but you can be as creative as you like here.

I saw a recipe that used mint extract and chopped bird's eye chilies as flavor, with chopped almonds as decoration. Another one used gin and tonic as a flavor (30ml gin and 60ml tonic reduced by boiling to 30ml) and added lemon and lime zest to the chocolate coating.

Magic Chocolate-Kaluha-Mint Truffles

Materials:
- Glass or ceramic mixing bowl
- Rubber/silicone spatula
- Whisky
- Small pot
- Melon baller
- Ice cream scoop
- Sheet pans
- Wax paper

Ingredients:
- 65g dry mushrooms or truffles, ground into a fine powder (use a coffee grinder for this)
- 20 oz + 4 oz (24 oz total) semi-sweet chocolate

---

[12] https://mycotopia.net/topic/39551-how-to-make-magic-chocolate-truffles (accessed January 23, 2019)

- 6 tbsp unsalted butter
- 1 cup heavy cream
- 2 tbsp light corn syrup
- 1/2 c Kaluha
- 1/4 tsp mint extract
- Lots of rainbow sprinkles (or cocoa powder, coconut flakes, finely chopped nuts)
- 12 oz bittersweet chocolate

Yield:
- 65 truffles (hence the use of 65g of mushrooms, so 1 truffle = 1 gram. Increase the proportion of mushrooms as you desire.)

Method:
Make the truffle balls

1. Line your trays with wax paper.
2. Pour the cream and syrup into the small pot and bring to a simmer over medium heat.
3. Put the butter and 20 oz semi-sweet chocolate in your glass mixing bowl. Microwave for three 30-second intervals, stirring with a spatula between each interval. This will soften up the chocolate a bit.
4. Pour the heated cream mix over the chocolate mix to fully melt the chocolate.
5. Stir in circles to make sure the mix is smooth and creamy.
6. Now, add the 1/2 c Kaluha and 1/4 tsp mint extract and stir some more.
7. Add the mushroom powder. Use a whisk to get it properly mixed in.

8. Cover the mixture with foil and place in the fridge for an hour or two until it is firm enough to scoop balls out with a melon baller.
9. Scoop out the balls and line them up on the waxed pans. Try to get 65 truffle balls out of the bowl, so that you will have 1 gram of mushroom in each truffle.
10. Place your trays back in the freezer for about 5 minutes to harden. Take them out and roll each truffle ball between your palms, or smooth them with your fingers, to form little balls. Then put back into the freezer.

Add the chocolate shell and topping

1. While the truffles are chilling, place the bittersweet chocolate and the last 4 oz of semi-sweet chocolate in a small bowl.
2. Microwave this chocolate at 30 second intervals, stirring very thoroughly between each interval, until the chocolate is JUST melted. Be careful here - if the temp goes above 94 F, the shell will not have that nice "SNAP" to it when you bite into the truffle. So heat the chocolate just enough to melt it. About 2 minutes tops are enough. Even if the chocolate doesn't look melted, if you stir it a lot, it will melt quickly. Basically, you want the temp to be just below body temp (90-92 F).
3. Pour sprinkles into another small bowl (or put different toppings into different bowls)
4. Dip your ice cream scoop into the melted chocolate to coat it.

5. Place a truffle ball into the scoop. Use your fingers or a fork to roll the truffle ball around in the melted chocolate to coat it all over.
6. Put your sprinkles and/or other toppings into small bowls and roll the truffle balls in them to cover them with the topping.
7. Once covered, place onto a new sheet of waxed paper on the pans and put back into the freezer to harden up. This doesn't take long at all, since the core is very cold.
8. Once completely frozen, you can put all the truffles in a container and store in the freezer for as long as you like. Keep those you plan to eat soon in the fridge.

SOME FINAL THOUGHTS ON CONSUMPTION

It's good news that eating magic mushrooms can be a tasty experience too! If you need some inspiration Google "magic mushrooms recipes" and see what comes up.

Just remember that you must remain mindful of dosages and potency.

RESOURCES AND ACKNOWLEDGEMENT

Although this book is extensive, it is far from containing all there is to know about mushrooms. You can find loads of different cultivation techniques, growers forums, tips and tricks, and all sort of useful tidbits if you have a look. Here are just a few of the resources which we would recommend:

Beug M, Bigwood J. "Quantitative analysis of psilocybin and psilocin in Psilocybe baeocystic Singer and Smith by high-performance liquid chromatography and by thin-layer chromatography." Journal of Chromatography 1981

Beug M, Bigwood J. "Variation of psilocybin and psilocin levels with repeated flushes (harvests) of mature sporocaps of Psilocybe cubensis (earle) Singer." Journal of Ethnopharmacology 1982.

Beug M, Bigwood J. "Psilocybin and psilocin levels in twenty species from seven genera of wild mushrooms in the Pacific Northwest (USA)" Journal of Ethnopharmacology 1982

Chang, Shu-Ting, and Philip G. Miles. "Edible Mushrooms and Their Cultivation. " CRC Press, 1989

Gartz and Muller. "analyses and cultivation of fruitbodies and mycelia of Psilocybe bohemica." Biochem Physiol Pflanzen. 1989

Griffiths RR, Richards WA, McCann U, Jesse R., "Psilocybin can occasion mystical-type experiences having substantial and sustained personal meaning and spiritual significance.", 2006

Heim RA, Hofmann A. "La psilocybine et la psilocine chez les psilocybe et strophaires hallucinogenes." Les champignons hallucinogenes du Mexique. 1958. Editions du Museum National d'Histoire Naturelle.

Mandrake, Dr. K and Haze, V. "The Psilocybin Mushroom Bible: The Definitive Guide to Growing and Using Magic Mushrooms", Green Candy Press, 2016

Nicholas, L. G., Ogamé, K."Psilocybin Mushroom Handbook: Easy Indoor and Outdoor Cultivation", Quick American, 2006

Oss, O.T. , and o.N. Oerie. "Psilocybin: Magic Mushroom Grower's Guide: A Handbook for Psilocybin Enthusiasts. " Quick American Publishing Company, 1992

Principium Quaesitor "Magic Mushroom Grower's Guide Simple Steps to Bulk Cultivation", The Psychonautical Society, 2015

Repke D, Leslie D, Guzman G. "Baeocystin in Psilocybie, Conocybe, and Panaeolus." LLoydia. 1977

Ronald F. Griffiths, Matthew W. Johnson, William A. Richards, "Psilocybin occasioned mystical-type experiences: immediate and persisting dose-related effects", 2011

Stamets P., Weil M.D. A."Psilocybin Mushrooms of the World: An Identification Guide.", Ten Speed Press, 2016

Stamets P, Beug PM, Bigwood J, Guzman G. "a new species and a new variety of Psilocybe from North America" Mycotaxon 1980

Stamets and Gartz. "a new caerulescent Psilocybe from the Pacitic Coast of Northwestern North America". Integration 6. 1995

Stivje, de Meijer. "Macromycetes from the state of Parana, Brazil. 4 The psychoactive species" Arq Biol Technol 1993

WEBISTE (SOME ARE COMMERCIAL SITES)

- Erowid.org
- Fanaticus.com
- Freshcapmushroom.com
- Howtousepsychedelics.org
- Myctopia.net
- Milkwood.net
- Mushmagic.com
- Mushworld.com
- Myctopia.net
- Mycomasters.com
- Psilosophy.info
- Psychedelicreview.com
- Shroomery.org
- Shroomology.org
- Zamnesia.com
- Thethirdwave.co
- Tripsafe.org
- Trufflemagic.com

ABOUT THE AUTHORS

Israel Bouseman grew up in South Florida, in a place lovingly described by some as the "mushroom capital of the world." In his youth, he was taught how to find psilocybin mushrooms in the wild, as well as how to harvest, cure, and prepare them in a number of different ways.

Israel studied the nature of the psychedelic experience and many tribal and modern perspectives on the navigation of the trip for many years prior to his first experience. Since then, he has been exploring the use of the psychedelics for healing, learning, and self-development for more than two decades. He also acts as a facilitator from time to time, creating a safe space for inexperienced journeyers to have a positive and constructive journey.

Hank Bryant comes from the opposite end of the United States, growing up in Maine. His first contact with the psilocybin mushroom was during his time in university. This is when his interest in  psychedelics began, and when he started to read everything he could find about the psilocybin mushroom. Cultivating mushrooms over two decades he wants to share his knowledge and spread the word about that wonderful tool.

Printed in Great Britain
by Amazon

86039308R00155